SPEEDY MOB

 KITCHEN

PHOTOGRAPHY BY DAVID LOFTUS

PAVILION

First published in the United Kingdom in 2020 by
Pavilion
43 Great Ormond Street
London WC1N 3HZ

ISBN 978-1-91164-183-4

A CIP catalogue record for this book is available from the
British Library

10 9 8 7 6 5 4 3 2 1

Reproduction by Rival Colour Ltd., UK
Printed and bound by 1010 Printing International Ltd, China

www.pavilionbooks.com

Publisher: Helen Lewis
Editor: Cara Armstrong
Copy Editor: Alice Sambrook
Design Manager: Laura Russell
Design Consultants: OMSE
Photographer: David Loftus
Props Stylist: Charlie Phillips
Food Stylists: Elena Silcock and Kitty Coles
Production Manager: Phil Brown

INTRODUCING...

A MOB CLASSIC

BEST PUDDING

SPOTIFY

When you see one of these Spotify Codes,
you scan it using the Spotify app to listen to
the corresponding playlist/song.

 VEGGIE

 VEGAN

WELCOME...

to speedy MOB. Since starting MOB Kitchen in 2016, we've had one consistent piece of feedback on our recipes: the MOB love the quick ones. Making a slow-roast leg of lamb or a butternut squash lasagne is all well and good at the weekend when you've got loads of time. However, the real challenge comes when you need a rapid breakfast before leaving the house. A quick lunch. Dinner after a long day at work when you've got mates coming over and you're so tired you can't be bothered. With this in mind, we decided to sit down and write our fastest ever book with recipes that can be made in 12 minutes or less. This is the definitive bible for quick cooking and we are so proud of it.

It's important to note here that this book doesn't stick to the 'under £10' promise of the first two books. It is primarily about speed. That being said, every recipe has been created with affordability in mind. While some recipes do call for slightly more expensive ingredients (steak, prawns, salmon, etc.), the majority of dishes in this book can be cooked on a shoestring.

So... why 12 minutes? Well, firstly it beats Jamie Oliver by 3 minutes. But also, it allows us to use ingredients like pasta and gnocchi, as well as providing enough time to flash-fry fish and meat and to knock up quick sauces and salads. But this isn't a casual cooking experience. There's no lounging around the kitchen chatting if you want to get it done in 12 minutes. It was a massive challenge getting every recipe in under time, but with lots of chopping and changing, we have nailed it. All the recipes in this book have been tested numerous times in order to shave seconds off the clock without compromising on the bold flavours crucial to every MOB recipe.

Along the way, we picked up a massive amount of time hacks, which you'll find throughout the book. We have also included a 'get ready' list of things to preheat and basic equipment to have on hand, specific to each recipe.

This isn't your average cook-along. We aren't saying that this is a relaxed cooking experience. It is intense, and you'll have to make use of all the hacks we've learnt in order to complete the 12-minute challenge. First things first. Game plan...

EQUIPMENT LISTS

POTS AND PANS, ETC.
- Two large frying pans (skillets), preferably non-stick
- Large measuring jug (pitcher)
- Large baking tray
- Large and small saucepans
- Large and small bowls for mixing
- Sieve and/or colander
- High-sided frying pan/casserole pan (this could be one of your large frying pans)
- A lid. If you don't have one for your pan, then use a baking tray to cover instead

FANCY
- Mini food processor with stick blender attachment (only needed for 7 recipes)
- Scales – crucial for 1 recipe only If you don't have them it's fine

SMALLER UTENSILS
- Wooden spoon
- Box grater
- Garlic crusher
- Sharp knife
- Chopping board
- Tin opener
- Tongs
- Scissors
- Ladle
- Whisk
- Peeler
- Fish slice/spatula
- Mug
- Tablespoon
- Teaspoon
- Fork
- Cutlery knife

TIME-SAVING HACKS

01   Get it all out. No searching for smoked paprika halfway through the recipe – there isn't time for that. This is the 12-minute challenge. Have all your equipment and ingredients out before you start, right down to the plates you are going to eat off.

02   Read. Not to be majorly patronizing, but make sure you read the whole recipe first.

03   Multitask. Such a small amount of time requires doing two things at once. With most of these recipes you will have one thing cooking in the background while you get on with making something else, or rope in a mate to help – your call.

04   Use your hands. Wherever possible, we've tried to eliminate steps to make things quicker, and that includes unnecessary chopping. Jarred roasted peppers can be torn straight into the pan. Fresh herbs like parsley and basil can be torn straight into dishes.

05   A box grater and garlic crusher are your friends. Use the coarse side to grate cheese or onions, or the fine side for ginger and garlic. Crush unpeeled garlic straight into the pan.

06   High heat. Don't be scared to whack the heat up high. We want a fast cook in order to get colour and caramelization – which is where all the flavour is at. Don't forget to give whatever is frying a quick poke around every now and again. We want colour not carnage. If you can, invest in two large non-stick frying pans – it will be a game changer.

07   Boil the kettle and turn on the oven or grill (broiler) before you start. That initial heat saves precious minutes. You'll find any preheating instructions at the top of the 'get ready' list on each recipe.

08   Keep it lean. You will find that most of the protein in this book, aside from cured meat, is lean just because it is going to cook quicker.

09   Go green. This book has lots of meat-free recipes in it. As you'll know from the MOB Veggie book, we enjoy eating this way. Cooking with veg also happens to be quick. Leafier vegetables are key for speed, no starchy roots here as they take too much time.

10   Use more sauces. Salsa verde, chimichurri, miso ginger, satay, tahini, the freshest yogurts – these dressings add massive amounts of flavour to your cooking, quickly.

11   Embrace shortcuts. To cut down on time throughout the book, we've used ready-made shortcuts such as pre-cooked pouches of rice, grains and lentils, all-in-one spice pastes and flavour-packers such as kimchi and jarred jalapeños. Everything we have chosen is about maximizing taste, not scrimping on quality.

12   Invest in a basic mini food processor with a stick blender attachment. This multi-purpose piece of kit is super useful and inexpensive.

BRUNCH

DISHES FOR EVERY OCCASION. ELEVATING YOUR BREAKFAST GAME

1

···|·||·||||·|···|·|·

Mary Clark
Take Me I'm Yours

V

SERVES 4

HUEVOS RANCHEROS

INGREDIENTS
2 x 400-g (14-oz) tins of black
  beans
1 tbsp ground cumin
1 tbsp smoked paprika
250 g (9 oz) cherry tomatoes
2 avocados
2 limes
4 UK medium (US large) eggs
  (we use British Lion)
4 soft corn tortillas
200-g (7-oz) block of feta
  (check the label if cooking
  veggie and find an alternative
  if needed)
hot sauce
olive oil
salt and black pepper

GET READY
saucepan
tin opener
sieve
tablespoon
wooden spoon
sharp knife
chopping board
large frying pan (skillet)
fish slice/spatula
4 serving plates

This Mexican-style breakfast 'ranchers eggs' is a biggie. Always look for the Red Lion mark on eggs bought in the UK as it symbolises the highest standards of food quality and safety. Keep your eggs in the fridge and get cracking!

01 Get a saucepan over a high heat and drizzle in some olive oil. Open and drain the tins of black beans into a sieve, then tip the beans straight into the pan. Refill one of the tins a quarter full with water and add to the pan. Add the cumin, smoked paprika and a good amount of salt and black pepper. Chuck in the tomatoes and give everything a good stir. Leave to cook for about 5 minutes, stirring occasionally, until the tomatoes have burst and the beans have broken down slightly.

02 Halve and pit the avocados, scoop out the flesh and slice it. Cut one lime in half and the other into four wedges. Squeeze one lime half over the avo slices and the other into the black beans.

03 Put a large frying pan over a high heat. Drizzle in some oil and, once hot, crack in the eggs. Fry to your liking.

04 Warm the tortillas in the microwave following the packet instructions. Place one tortilla on each serving plate. Spoon over the tomatoey beans, then top each one with half a sliced avocado and a fried egg. Crumble over the feta and serve with the remaining lime wedges for squeezing over and some hot sauce.

SPEED HACK
Chuck whole cherry tomatoes in with the spiced black beans, for less chopping and saucier refried beans.

The Magic Lantern
Holding Hands

[V]

SERVES 4

SPEEDIEST CHIPOTLE SHAKSHUKA

*TAKE A PHOTO AND SHARE YOUR SHAK WITH THE MOB

#FEEDTHEMOB

The ultimate hangover cure – saucy, smoky, spicy eggs. Serve our speediest ever shakshuka straight out of the pan so everyone can get stuck in.

INGREDIENTS
600-g (1 lb 5-oz) jar of passata (strained tomatoes)
1–2 tbsp chipotle paste
450-g (1-lb) jar of roasted red (bell) peppers
8 UK medium (US large) eggs
1 pack of pitta breads
natural yogurt
1 small bunch fresh parsley
olive oil
salt and black pepper

GET READY
large frying pan (skillet)
tablespoon
fork
wooden spoon
large lid
serving bowl
spoon
4 serving plates

01 Get a large frying pan over a high heat. Drizzle in some olive oil, then empty the passata straight into the pan. Add 1–2 tablespoons of chipotle paste (to your taste), then pick out the roasted peppers with a fork, leaving their juices behind, and tear into the pan. Give everything a stir and season with salt and black pepper. Let bubble away for 1 minute.

02 Crack the eggs into the pan and season with salt and black pepper, then cover with a lid. Cook for 4–5 minutes, until the whites are just set but the yolks are still runny.

03 Meanwhile, toast the pitta breads, tear into pieces and put into a serving bowl.

04 Once the eggs are cooked, dollop over spoonfuls of the natural yogurt, scatter over the parsley and serve at the table with extra black pepper and the pitta breads for dunking.

SPEED HACK
Chipotle paste. It packs a complex flavour punch in one quick spoonful so you don't need anything else.

MOB Time:
12 mins, 00 secs

Bongmaster Inc
Brothers & Sisters

V

SERVES 4

DIY BEETROOT SABICH

INGREDIENTS
4 UK medium (US large) eggs
1 red onion
2 tbsp red wine vinegar
1 tsp caster (superfine) sugar
8 pitta breads
250-g (9-oz) pack of cooked beetroot (not in vinegar)
1 small bunch fresh parsley
1 tub of hummus
chilli sauce
salt

GET READY
boil the kettle
saucepan
sharp knife
chopping board
4 serving bowls
tablespoon
sieve
5 serving plates

Mezze meets ultimate pitta pocket. The quick pickled red onions are a game changer here. Make sure you properly scrunch them with your hands so that they soften faster.

01 Pour the boiling water into a saucepan over a medium heat and bring back to the boil. Add the eggs and set a timer for 6½ minutes (for soft-boiled).

02 Meanwhile, slice the red onion as thinly as you can and then scrape into a bowl. Add the red wine vinegar, sugar, a good pinch of salt and a splash of hot water. Stir together with a spoon to incorporate all the ingredients. Scrunch the onion with your hands in the liquid to encourage it to soften. Set aside to quick pickle.

03 Put the pitta breads on to toast. Open and drain the pack of beetroot, slice the beetroot and scrape into a bowl. Tear the parsley into another bowl. Put the toasted pittas into a third bowl.

04 Drain the soft-boiled eggs, then put into a sieve and rinse under cold water until cool enough to handle. Peel the eggs, cut them in half and plate up.

05 Lay all the components out for the sabich, including hummus and chilli sauce, for people to help themselves.

SPEED HACK
Sabich, an Israeli street food sandwich, is classically made with fried aubergine (eggplant). Here, we've swapped the aubergine for ready-cooked beetroot – an equally good friend to hummus.

HOT PITTA IS
CRUCIAL SO MAKE
SURE YOU'VE GOT
EVERYTHING READY

MOB Time:
11 mins, 59 secs

Tomppabeats
Monday Loop

SERVES 4

MOB'S SPEEDY FRY UP

The speediest fry up you'll ever cook, guaranteed. The key here is high heat and some good multitasking. Get into the zone and smash it in 12 minutes – you may need to enlist the MOB to help.

INGREDIENTS

12 pork chipolata sausages
8 rashers streaky bacon
250 g (9 oz) button
  mushrooms
250 g (9 oz) cherry tomatoes
6 UK large (US extra-large)
  eggs
knob (pat) of butter
4 large slices of bread
  of your choice
condiments of your choice
olive oil
salt and black pepper

GET READY

2 large frying pans (skillets)
sharp knife
chopping board
tongs
large measuring jug (pitcher)
fork
5 serving plates

01 Get two large frying pans over a high heat and drizzle a little oil into each. Place the chipolatas in one of the pans. Space out the rashers of bacon in the other.

02 Roughly chop the mushrooms, then chuck them into the pan with the bacon. Nestle the cherry tomatoes between the sausages in the pan. Fry for about 8 minutes, turning the sausages and bacon when needed, until everything is cooked through and to your liking. Turn down the heat on the bacon pan if it is crisp before the sausages are done.

03 Meanwhile, crack the eggs into a large measuring jug. Whisk together with a fork and season well with salt and black pepper. Add a knob of butter. Blast in the microwave for 30 seconds at a time, stirring after each blast, until you have super creamy scrambled eggs. Stop cooking just before the eggs are set as they will carry on cooking in the jug.

04 Toast the bread and put it onto a plate. Serve the sausages, tomatoes, bacon, mushrooms, scrambled eggs and toast at the table, with plenty of condiments for people to help themselves.

SPEED HACK

Make the scrambled eggs in the microwave while everything else is frying. Check and mix them every 30 seconds and be sure to take them out of the microwave when they are still a little runny.

MOB Time:
11 mins, 48 secs

Cassia
100 Times Over

SERVES 4

TALEGGIO, HAM & CORNICHON BAKED CROISSANTS

A GREAT DISH FOR WHEN YOU'RE ON THE GO

INGREDIENTS
200 g (7 oz) Taleggio cheese
cornichons
4 large croissants
wholegrain mustard
1 packet of ham of your choice
  (we like honey-roasted)

GET READY
preheat the oven to 180°C fan
  (200°C/400°F/Gas Mark 6)
sharp knife
chopping board
large baking tray
cutlery knife
4 serving plates

We've given some oomph to the classic French ham and cheese croissant with a lick of mustard, tangy Taleggio cheese and pickled cornichons. It may be bastardized, but it's a banger.

01 Cut the Taleggio cheese into 12 slices and thinly slice some cornichons. Cut each croissant in half and place on a baking tray.

02 Spread the bottom half of each croissant with some wholegrain mustard, then pile on the ham, cheese slices and a few cornichon slices. Place on the top half of each croissant.

03 Bake in the oven for 7–8 minutes until the cheese is melted and the croissants are crisp. Game changer.

SPEED HACK
Whack the oven on before you do anything else. Assemble the croissants, production-line style, on the baking tray ready for the oven.

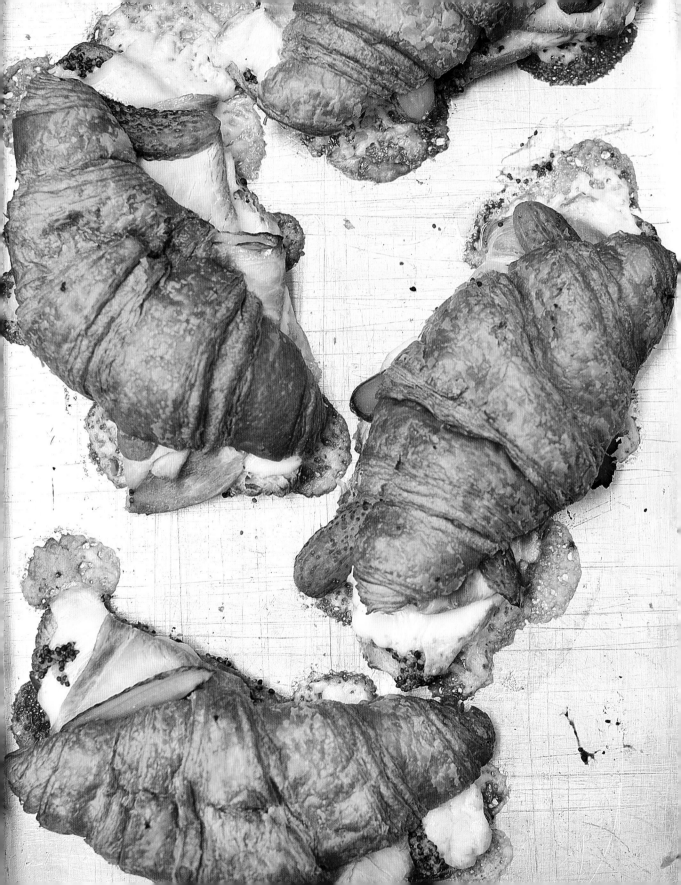

MOB Time:
10 mins, 17 secs

Theo Lawrence & The Hearts
Search Your Heart

SERVES 4

'NDUJA PESTO SCRAMBLED EGGS

OUR FAVOURITE BRUNCH IN THE BOOK

INGREDIENTS

8 UK large (US extra-large)
  eggs
3 tbsp 'nduja pesto
butter
8 slices of crusty bread
  (sourdough or multigrain)
small bag of rocket (arugula)
  or mixed leaves
sherry vinegar
salt and black pepper

GET READY

large measuring jug (pitcher)
fork/whisk
tablespoon
large frying pan (skillet)
wooden spoon
4 serving plates
cutlery knife

No milk here MOB. The secret to perfectly silky scrambled eggs is a big knob of butter, not stirring the eggs constantly and taking them off the heat before they are done.

01 Crack the eggs into a large measuring jug. Whisk to combine the whites and yolks, then add the 'nduja pesto along with some salt and black pepper. Whisk again.

02 Get a large frying pan over a medium heat. Add a knob (pat) of butter and wait until it's melted, then pour in the 'nduja pesto eggs. Stir the eggs, moving your spoon through the entire pan, every 20 seconds or so until you end up with big pieces of silky, slightly runny scrambled eggs.

03 Meanwhile, start toasting the bread and put it straight onto plates as it's done.

04 Take the pan of eggs off the heat while the eggs are still a bit runny as they will carry on cooking in the pan.

05 Butter the toast, then spoon over the scrambled eggs. Top each portion with a pile of rocket and a small splash of sherry vinegar.

SPEED HACK

'Nduja pesto takes these scrambled eggs to the next level in the simplest way possible. Whisk 3 tablespoons straight into the eggs for that spicy kick you know you want.

MOB Time:
11 mins, 43 secs

Sammy Rae
Saw It Coming

SERVES 4

PARMA HAM-WRAPPED ASPARAGUS SOLDIERS & EGGS

INGREDIENTS
300 g (10½ oz) asparagus spears
2 packets of Parma ham
8 UK medium (US large) eggs
Tabasco
olive oil
salt and black pepper

GET READY
preheat the grill (broiler)
  to maximum
boil the kettle
large baking tray
large saucepan
sieve
8 egg cups or shot glasses
4 serving plates

A worldie of a combo – nothing beats jammy boiled eggs served with tender, sweet asparagus wrapped in crisp, salty Parma ham. This dish is at its best when asparagus is in season.

01 Wrap two asparagus spears in one slice of Parma ham and put on a large baking tray. Repeat for the rest of the asparagus and ham and toss any extra asparagus onto the baking tray too. Drizzle with a little olive oil and place under the hot grill for 7–8 minutes.

02 Meanwhile, pour the boiling water from the kettle into a large saucepan over a medium heat and bring back to the boil. Add the eggs and set a timer for 6 minutes.

03 Drain the boiled eggs into a sieve, then put the eggs into egg cups or shot glasses on four plates. Divide the ham and asparagus soldiers between plates. Serve with Tabasco and salt and pepper.

SPEED HACK
Wrap two asparagus spears each in one piece of Parma ham. Don't worry about any stray spears, just grill them without ham.

MOB Time:
10 mins, 11 secs

🟢 ⥾|⥾|⥾|⥾⥾⥾|⥾|⥾⥾|⥾⥾|⥾⥾|⥾

Gil Scott Heron
Gun

SERVES 4

HAM HOCK, FRIED EGG, WATERCRESS & PICCALILLI ROLLS

INGREDIENTS

large knob (pat) of butter
4 crusty rolls of your choice
  (we like seeded or ciabatta)
piccalilli
4 UK medium (US large) eggs
2 packets of shredded
  ham hock
1 packet of watercress
salt and black pepper

GET READY

large frying pan (skillet)
sharp knife
chopping board
cutlery knife
4 serving plates
fish slice/spatula

The naughtiest little breakfast roll you'll ever munch. The tanginess of the piccalilli cuts through the richness of the buttery fried egg and shredded ham hock.

01 Get a large frying pan over a high heat and add the butter.

02 While the butter is melting, slice open the rolls and spread piccalilli on both halves. Place on serving plates.

03 Crack the eggs into the frying pan and season with salt and black pepper. Fry to your liking.

04 Pile some ham hock into each roll and place a fried egg on top of each. Pour a little melted butter from the pan over each egg and top each roll with watercress to finish.

SPEED HACK

Slice the rolls and spread with piccalilli while the butter is melting in the pan. This has the added bonus of browning the butter slightly, giving a rich, nutty flavour to the fried eggs.

RUNNY YOLK IS
KING IN THIS DISH

MOB Time:
11 mins, 03 secs

Joy Crookes
Mother May I Sleep with Danger?

SERVES 4

SMOKED MACKEREL KEDGEREE

INGREDIENTS
4 UK medium (US large) eggs
  (we use British Lion)
1 red onion
thumb-sized piece of fresh
  ginger
2 tbsp curry powder
2 x 250-g (9-oz) pouches of
  pre-cooked long-grain rice
300 g (10½ oz) frozen peas
4 smoked mackerel fillets
1 lemon
1 small bunch fresh coriander
  (cilantro)
olive oil
salt and black pepper

GET READY
boil the kettle
small saucepan
large frying pan (skillet)
grater
tablespoon
wooden spoon
sieve
sharp knife
chopping board
4 serving bowls

Fish for brunch? Feels weird but trust us, once you've tried this classic combo you won't look back. It is the kind of food you want when you are run-down. Filling, warming and a little bit spicy.

01 Pour the boiling water into a saucepan over a medium heat. Add the eggs and set a timer for 6½ minutes (for soft-boiled).

02 Meanwhile, get a large frying pan over a high heat and drizzle in a decent amount of oil. Peel the red onion, then coarsely grate the onion and the ginger directly into the pan. Add the curry powder and cook, stirring, for 1 minute.

03 Squeeze the unopened rice pouches with your hands to separate the grains a bit, then open and tip into the pan along with a decent splash of boiling water. Add the frozen peas, stir and cook for a minute to defrost the peas.

04 Peel the skin off the mackerel and flake into the pan. Turn the heat down low, season with salt and pepper and leave to heat through.

05 Drain the eggs, place in a sieve and run under cold water until cool enough to handle. Peel the eggs and cut in half. Cut the lemon into four wedges. Top the kedgeree in the pan with the egg halves, lemon wedges and torn coriander. Serve straight from the pan into bowls.

SPEED HACK
The humble box grater. Use the coarse side to grate the onion straight into the pan and the fine side for the ginger.

HNNY
Cheer Up, My Brother

SERVES 4

SCATTER WITH EXTRA CHILLI FLAKES IF YOU LIKE IT HOT

SAAG PANEER & PEA FRITTATA

The flavours of saag paneer in a frittata? It's a 10/10. One for the meal prep MOB – this is a great meal to take for lunch the next day. Serve with plenty of mango chutney and hot sauce.

INGREDIENTS

1 tbsp curry powder
2 tsp cumin seeds
2 tsp dried chilli flakes (hot red pepper flakes)
225-g (8-oz) block of paneer
200 g (7 oz) baby leaf spinach
150 g (5½ oz) frozen peas
8 UK large (US extra-large) eggs
mango chutney
hot sauce
neutral oil, such as groundnut
salt and black pepper

GET READY

preheat the grill (broiler) to maximum
large ovenproof frying pan (skillet)
tablespoon and teaspoon
grater
wooden spoon
measuring jug (pitcher)
fork
4 serving plates

01 Get a large ovenproof frying pan over a high heat. Drizzle in a good glug of neutral oil. Add the curry powder, cumin seeds and chilli flakes. Coarsely grate the paneer straight into the pan. Fry, stirring, for 30 seconds to coat the cheese in the spices. Tip the spinach and peas into the pan.

02 While the spinach is wilting, crack the eggs into a measuring jug and whisk with a fork to combine the whites and yolks. Season with salt and black pepper.

03 Come back to the frying pan and give everything a good stir. Season with salt and black pepper.

04 Pour the eggs into the pan and swirl the pan to level out the eggs. Fry for 2 minutes without stirring, then whack under the hot grill for 5 minutes until cooked through. Serve at the table out of the pan with mango chutney and hot sauce.

SPEED HACK
Coarsely grate the paneer straight into the pan. This saves so much time and it means the cheese gets fully coated in the spices.

SARNIES, BAGELS & TOAST

SOME OF THE FRESHEST SANDWICHES YOU'LL EVER MAKE

2

MOB Time:
11 mins, 43 secs

 ·|·|¦¦¦||¦|¦·¦¦|·

Slim Young
Otan Hunu

SERVES 4

SPEEDIEST FISH FINGER SARNIES

INGREDIENTS
2 baby gem lettuces
malt vinegar
4 skinless and boneless white
   fish fillets (haddock or cod)
6 tbsp mayonnaise
½ packet of panko
   breadcrumbs
2 tbsp capers
8 slices of bread (seeded,
   white or wholemeal/
   whole-wheat)
olive oil
salt and black pepper

GET READY
sharp knife
chopping board
large bowl
2 large frying pans (skillets)
tablespoon
tongs
small bowl
4 serving plates

A proper fish finger sarnie is a thing of beauty. We've used malt vinegar to pep up the lettuce and in our speedy riff on a tartare sauce. For the crispiest, flakiest fish fingers, make sure to get the oil in both frying pans piping hot before you start frying.

01 Slice up the baby gem lettuces and put in a large bowl. Drizzle over a little malt vinegar. Set aside.

02 Get two large frying pans over a medium-high heat. Drizzle in enough oil to just coat the base of each pan.

03 Cut the fish fillets into finger-sized pieces. Season on the chopping board with salt and black pepper, then dollop over 2 tablespoons of the mayo. Use your hands to gently toss the fish pieces so that each finger is evenly coated in the mayo. Shake over enough breadcrumbs to cover the fish and use your hands to stick the crumbs to the fish pieces on all sides.

04 Place the fish fingers into the hot pans in a single layer. Fry for 2–3 minutes, turning occasionally, until they are crisp and golden on all sides.

05 Meanwhile, dollop the remaining 4 tablespoons of mayo into a small bowl. Add the capers, stir and season with malt vinegar and salt and black pepper to taste. Quick tartare sauce – done.

06 Build your sarnies onto four plates. Spread a spoonful of tartare sauce on the bottom slices of bread, add lettuce, the fish fingers and more sauce to taste. Add the sandwich tops and boom.

SPEED HACK
Fish fingers without the hassle of the three-bowl, flour, egg and breadcrumb coating business. Cut the fish into fingers, then coat with mayo and sprinkle over the breadcrumbs while they're still on the chopping board.

BE GENEROUS WITH THE VINEGAR

MOB Time:
11 mins, 03 secs

Sonny Okosun
Mother & Child

SERVES 4

CURRIED COCONUT CHICKPEAS ON TOAST

INGREDIENTS
3 x 400-g (14-oz) tins of
   chickpeas
coconut oil
2 garlic cloves
thumb-sized piece of fresh
   ginger
2 tbsp curry powder
8 slices of sourdough bread
350-g (12-oz) pot of coconut
   yogurt
2 limes
1 tbsp nigella seeds
1 small bunch fresh coriander
   (cilantro)
salt and black pepper

GET READY
tin opener
sieve
large frying pan (skillet)
tablespoon
grater
wooden spoon
sharp knife
chopping board
4 serving plates

Imagine Indian-style beans on toast. This is what you get with this saucy little curried chickpea number, with creamy coconut yogurt, fresh ginger, garlic and lime. This will become your go-to for a lazy dinner.

01   Open the tins of chickpeas, drain into a sieve and rinse with fresh water. Leave in the sieve to drain again while you make the base of the curry.

02   Get a large frying pan over a low heat and dollop in a generous tablespoon of coconut oil. While it is melting, finely grate the garlic cloves and ginger straight into the pan. Turn up the heat to high and add the curry powder. Fry for 1 minute, stirring, to cook out the spices.

03   Tip in the chickpeas and give everything a good mix. Leave to fry, stirring occasionally, while you toast the sourdough bread.

04   Empty the coconut yogurt into the pan, then half-fill the pot with water and pour that in too and mix everything together. Bring to the boil and let the chickpeas bubble away in the creamy sauce for a minute or two. Season with salt and black pepper to taste.

05   Cut one lime into four wedges and the other lime in half. Squeeze the juice of the halved lime over the chickpeas in the pan, then scatter over the nigella seeds and tear over the coriander.

06   Divide the toast between four plates and top with mounds of the curried chickpeas. Serve with the lime wedges on the side for squeezing over.

SPEED HACK
Using coconut yogurt rather than milk adds richness and means you don't have to spend ages reducing the sauce.

Noname
Self

V

SERVES 4

LOVELY TUNE

FRIED EGGS WITH SALSA VERDE ON TOAST

INGREDIENTS

1 large bunch fresh parsley
2 tbsp capers
1 small garlic clove
2 tsp Dijon mustard
4 tbsp extra virgin olive oil
1–2 tbsp red wine vinegar
8 slices of sourdough bread
8 UK medium (US extra-large)
  eggs
olive oil
salt and black pepper

GET READY

mini food processor
tablespoon and teaspoon
2 large frying pans (skillets)
fish slice/spatula
4 serving plates

Salsa verde is one of those genius sauces that makes everything taste more delicious. The richness of the fried egg is a marriage made in heaven with the tang of the capers, mustard and vinegar. Talk to me Veronica.

01 Salsa verde time. Put the parsley (stalks and all), capers and garlic clove into a mini food processor. Blitz until finely chopped, you may have to unpick the parsley stalks from the blade at first, but persist, they will break down. Once chopped, add the mustard, extra virgin olive oil, red wine vinegar and salt and black pepper to taste. Blitz briefly to combine. Salsa verde, done.

02 Start toasting your sourdough bread.

03 Meanwhile, get two large frying pans over a high heat. Drizzle in some oil, then crack in the eggs. Fry to your liking.

04 Divide the toast between four plates, top each slice with a fried egg and drizzle over the salsa verde to serve.

SPEED HACK
A mini food processor is your mate. No need for finely chopped parsley and garlic here – blitz the sauce in seconds.

Rose Mitchel
Baby Please Don't Go

V

SERVES 4

HARISSA TOMATO BRUSCHETTA

MAKE IT VEGAN BY USING COCONUT YOGURT INSTEAD

INGREDIENTS
8 slices of sourdough or
   crusty white bread
1 garlic clove
large pot of Greek yogurt
400 g (14 oz) cherry tomatoes
2–3 tbsp harissa paste
1 lemon
1 small bunch fresh basil
olive oil
salt and black pepper

GET READY
sharp knife
chopping board
spoon
4 serving plates
large frying pan (skillet)
tablespoon
wooden spoon
grater

MOB, this is our best ever bruschetta. Cherry tomatoes chucked in a hot frying pan with olive oil and fragrant harissa are fried until they just begin to burst, then spooned over cool yogurt and garlic toasts. Whammy.

01 Toast the bread. Meanwhile, peel the garlic clove. As each piece of toast is ready, rub it on one side with the garlic, then spread with a big spoonful of Greek yogurt and put onto plates.

02 Get a large frying pan over a super high heat and drizzle in a good glug of olive oil. Chuck in the cherry tomatoes and season with salt and black pepper. Fry for 2 minutes until the tomatoes just begin to burst. Stir in the harissa paste to taste, then remove from the heat.

03 Spoon the hot tomatoes over the cool yogurt toasts, making sure to spoon over all the flavoured oil from the pan too. Finely grate a little lemon zest over each plate of bruschetta and tear over a few basil leaves to finish.

SPEED HACK
Get everything ready with the toast and put on serving plates before you've even started frying the tomatoes.

MOB Time:
8 mins, 59 secs

Louis Berry
Molly Malone

SERVES 4

NEW YORK PASTRAMI BAGELS

CRISPS ARE CRUCIAL HERE FOR THE CRUNCH

INGREDIENTS

4 bagels of your choice
1 tbsp wholegrain mustard
5 tbsp mayonnaise
3 tomatoes
200-g (7-oz) block of Swiss cheese
4 gherkins (pickles)
1 baby gem lettuce
12 slices of pastrami
crisps
salt and black pepper

GET READY

tablespoon
small bowl
sharp knife
chopping board
4 serving plates

MOB's take on the New York classic with salt beef and pickles. We've added some mustard mayo, crunchy gem lettuce, juicy tomatoes and Swiss cheese. It's a freshy.

01   Start toasting the bagels.

02   Mix the mustard and mayo together in a small bowl. Slice the tomatoes into rounds and season them with salt and pepper.

03   Slice up the Swiss cheese. Slice the gherkins and separate the lettuce leaves.

04   Assembly time. Line up your toasted bagel bases and spread a layer of mustard mayo onto each. Top the bases with pastrami, the sliced tomatoes, cheese, pickles and lettuce. Sandwich on the bagel tops and eat with crisps.

SPEED HACK

Start toasting the bagels first. It may sound silly, but trust us, 8 separate bagel halves are going to take a while.

MOB Time:
12 mins, 00 secs

Kansas Smitty's
Whiskey Rag – Live

SERVES 4

SPICY SMOKED CHEDDAR TUNA MELTS

INGREDIENTS
3 spring onions (scallions)
2 x 160-g (5¾-oz) tins of tuna
    in spring water
mayonnaise
hot sauce
8 slices of sourdough bread
250 g (9 oz) smoked Cheddar
    cheese
salt and black pepper

GET READY
chopping board
sharp knife
tin opener
bowl
cutlery knife
spoon
grater
2 large frying pans (skillets)
fish slice/spatula
4 serving plates

We've perfected the classic using smoked Cheddar and hot sauce. Make sure you press your toasties down in the pan for ultimate ooziness.

01   Thinly slice the spring onions. Open the tins of tuna and drain off the water. Put the drained tuna meat and sliced spring onions in a bowl and add as much mayonnaise and hot sauce as you like. Season to taste with salt and black pepper and stir together.

02   Assembly time. Put four slices of sourdough bread onto a chopping board. Spread a thin layer of mayonnaise over each slice, then turn them mayo-side-down onto the board. Spoon the spicy tuna mayo evenly over each piece of bread, then grate the smoked Cheddar directly over the top of each one.

03   Top with the remaining bread slices and spread a thin layer of mayo on the top-facing side of each. (Having mayo on the outside of the bread is the answer to a super crisp toastie!)

04   Get two large frying pans, preferably non-stick, over a high heat. Fry the toasties for 1 minute on each side until golden, squashing them down with a fish slice or spatula as they cook for ultimate crispiness. Transfer to plates and serve.

SPEED HACK
Production line tactics. Spread all the bread with mayo, then assemble with filling and grate the cheese straight over the toasties. Use two frying pans: you need to cook all the toasties at once to beat the clock.

MOB Time:
11 mins, 45 secs

Kalabrese
Wanzka

SERVES 4

STEAK, MUSTARD & CARAMELIZED ONION BAGUETTES

INGREDIENTS
1 ½ tbsp Dijon mustard
4 tbsp mayonnaise
2 large baguettes
340 g (12 oz) beef medallion
  steaks
1 small bag of rocket (arugula)
sherry vinegar
caramelized red onion chutney
olive oil
salt and black pepper

GET READY
large frying pan (skillet)
tablespoon
small bowl
sharp knife
chopping board
tongs
cutlery knife
5 serving plates

There are some days when only a steak sandy will do. Add some peppery rocket, sweet caramelized onions and creamy mayo and you're onto a winner. We've upped the flavour even more by coating the steaks in Dijon mustard straight out the pan.

01 Get a large frying pan over a high heat and wait until it is searing hot – this will take a couple of minutes.

02 Meanwhile, mix 1 tablespoon of the mustard with the mayonnaise in a small bowl. Cut the baguettes in half lengthways.

03 Season the steaks liberally with salt and black pepper on both sides. Drizzle some olive oil into the hot frying pan. Once the oil is sizzling, add the steaks and fry for 2 minutes on each side.

04 Meanwhile, spread the remaining ½ tablespoon of mustard onto a plate. When the steaks are cooked, transfer to the plate and turn the steaks so that they get coated in mustard on both sides. Leave to rest while you assemble your sandwiches.

05 Spread the mustard mayo over the bottom half of each baguette, then pile on some rocket and drizzle over a bit of sherry vinegar. Slice the steaks, then pile on top of the rocket.

06 Spread caramelized red onion chutney over the top half of each baguette, sandwich on the top halves and cut each baguette in half. Steak sarnies, done.

SPEED HACK
Start assembling the sandwiches while the steak is resting. Make up two long baguettes, then cut them in half for four sandwiches.

Cody Chesnutt
Serve This Royalty

SERVES 4

WELSH RAREBIT

MOB'S TAKE
ON THE WELSH
CLASSIC - DONE
IN MINUTES

INGREDIENTS

8 large slices of crusty bread
   (white or sourdough are best)
350 g (12 oz) extra mature
   Cheddar cheese
2 UK large (US extra-large)
   eggs
1 tbsp English mustard
4 tbsp stout beer
Worcestershire sauce
black pepper

GET READY

preheat the grill (broiler)
   to maximum
large baking tray
grater
mixing bowl
tablespoon
4 serving plates

If you like cheese on toast and you have never made this, it is going to change your life. Grilled cheese is made richer and more complex with egg yolks, beer, mustard and Worcestershire sauce.

01 Put the bread on a large baking tray and toast under the grill until golden on both sides.

02 Meanwhile, coarsely grate the Cheddar cheese into a mixing bowl. Separate the eggs (discard the whites or keep and use them for something else), then add the yolks to the bowl with the cheese. Add the mustard and stout, shake in a few good drops of Worcestershire sauce and season with black pepper. Mix well.

03 Spoon the cheesy mixture over the toast, spread with the back of the spoon and return to the hot grill until the cheese is bubbling, melted and browned. Transfer to serving plates and finish with extra Worcestershire sauce. Ultimate cheese on toast – done.

SPEED HACK

Get the grill on before you start anything else. Toast the bread while you make the cheese mix.

SALADS
& BOWLS

3

FOR THE HEALTHY
MOB. SOME GREAT
SUMMER OPTIONS

MOB Time:
12 mins, 00 secs

Hallelujah Chicken Run Band
Kare Nanhasi

SERVES 4

NUTTY COUSCOUS TABBOULEH

INGREDIENTS
1 red onion
2 large lemons
250 g (9 oz) couscous
1 heaped tbsp ras el hanout
200 g (7 oz) mixed nuts
200 g (7 oz) dried apricots
1 small bunch fresh parsley
1 small bunch fresh mint
1 small bunch fresh coriander
  (cilantro)
1 cucumber
olive oil
salt

GET READY
boil the kettle
sharp knife
chopping board
small bowl
large serving bowl
tablespoon
clingfilm (plastic wrap)
spoon
frying pan (skillet)
fork
4 serving plates

The tastiest tabbouleh this side of Lebanon. With quick pickled onion, loads of toasty nuts, dried apricots and all the fresh herbs. Meal prep gold; take it with you for lunches the rest of the week.

01 Slice the red onion as thinly as you can and scrape into a small bowl. Cut the lemons in half.

02 Put the couscous into a large serving bowl. Add the ras el hanout and a good pinch of salt. Pour over enough boiling water to just cover the couscous and cover the bowl with clingfilm.

03 While the couscous is steaming, squeeze all the lemon juice over the red onion in the small bowl. Add a splash of hot water from the kettle and mix together with a spoon. Season with a good pinch of salt and scrunch the onion into the liquid with your hand. Leave to quick pickle.

04 Get a dry frying pan over a medium heat, tip in the mixed nuts and toast for 5 minutes, occasionally shaking the pan, then turn off the heat.

05 Meanwhile, roughly chop the apricots and then the parsley, mint and coriander. Slice the cucumber into half-moons.

06 Back to the couscous. Take off the clingfilm and use a fork to fluff up the grains. Drizzle in a couple of generous glugs of olive oil. Add the toasted nuts, cucumber, apricots, herbs and quick pickled onion along with the juices.

07 Give everything a mix, adjust the seasoning and add more olive oil if needed. Serve at the table for people to help themselves.

SPEED HACK
Multitasking: while you chop, the onions are pickling, the couscous is steaming and the nuts are in the pan having a toast.

MOB Time:
9 mins, 05 secs

Liam Bailey
When Will They Learn (Chase & Status Remix)

SERVES 4

THREE BEAN & SWEETCORN SALAD

INGREDIENTS

2 x 400-g (14-oz) tins of three beans in water (or 1 tin of white beans and 1 tin brown beans instead)
2 x 198-g (7-oz) tins of sweetcorn
4 spring onions (scallions)
2 limes
1 fat garlic clove
cayenne pepper
250 g (9 oz) cherry tomatoes
2 avocados
jarred jalapeños
bag of plain tortilla chips
olive oil
salt and black pepper

GET READY

tin opener
sieve
mixing bowl
sharp knife
chopping board
grater
teaspoon
4 serving plates

We've amped up the Mexican flavours in this three bean salad with a punchy garlic, lime and cayenne pepper dressing, spicy pickled jalapeños and crunchy tortilla chips.

01 Open the tins of beans, drain into a sieve and rinse with cold water. Shake off any excess water and tip into a mixing bowl. Open and drain the tinned sweetcorn and add to the beans.

02 Thinly slice the spring onions and cut the limes in half. Scrape the spring onions into the bowl with the beans and squeeze in the juice of three lime halves. Finely grate the garlic clove straight into the bowl. Add ½ teaspoon of cayenne pepper along with a good drizzle of olive oil. Mix well.

03 Squish the cherry tomatoes with your hands into the bowl. Season the salad with salt and black pepper to taste, adding extra oil and lime juice if needed, and stir. Pile onto four plates.

04 Halve and pit the avocados, scoop out the flesh and slice. Squeeze the remaining lime half over the avocado slices and divide between the salads. Sprinkle a little extra cayenne pepper over each salad and scatter over a few jalapeños. Crush a small handful of tortilla chips directly over each salad to finish. Banging.

SPEED HACK
Build the salad in the mixing bowl. The dressing gets made straight over the beans and the sweetcorn, then you keep on adding ingredients and layers of flavour.

Nick Drake
Saturday Sun

SERVES 4

TUSCAN ANTIPASTI BREAD SALAD

STALE BREAD ALSO WORKS

INGREDIENTS
3 ciabatta rolls
2 garlic cloves
1 large bag of rocket (arugula)
3 fresh antipasti pots of
   your choice (we like mixed
   vegetable antipasti,
   sun-dried tomatoes, olives
   or chargrilled artichokes)
200-g (7-oz) block of feta
   (check the label if cooking
   veggie and find an alternative
   if needed)
2–3 tbsp balsamic vinegar
olive oil
salt and black pepper

GET READY
large frying pan (skillet)
garlic crusher
tongs
large serving bowl
tablespoon
4 serving plates

One for the lazy MOB. This might well be the speediest recipe in the whole book. Choose a selection of your favourite supermarket antipasti pots, make some garlicky croutons and whack some rocket and feta in for good measure.

01 Get a large frying pan over a high heat and drizzle in a good glug of olive oil. Tear the ciabatta rolls into rough croutons straight into the pan. Crush in the unpeeled garlic cloves over the bread and season with salt and black pepper. Fry, turning the bread regularly with tongs, for around 3 minutes until it is crisp and golden. Take off the heat and set aside.

02 Tip the rocket and the antipasti pots (along with their oil) into a large serving bowl and toss together. Chuck in the croutons, crumble in the feta in large chunks and then pour in the balsamic vinegar to taste. Give everything a good mix. Season with salt and black pepper to taste, adding a splash more vinegar, if you like.

03 Divide the salad between four plates and serve.

SPEED HACK
No chopping required, this salad is all about using your hands. Tear the ciabatta straight into the pan for croutons, crumble up the feta and empty out the antipasti pots.

King Geedorah
Next Levels

SERVES 4

BEETROOT, BLUE CHEESE, CHICORY & WALNUT SALAD

INGREDIENTS
4 chicory
2 eating apples
2 x 250-g (9-oz) packs of
   cooked beetroot (not in
   vinegar)
2–3 pickled walnuts from a jar
200 g (7 oz) blue cheese
   (check the label if cooking
   veggie and find an alternative
   if needed)
1 crusty baguette
extra virgin olive oil
salt and black pepper

GET READY
4 serving plates
sharp knife
chopping board
fork
spoon

Pickled walnuts are one of those old school ingredients that aren't really used anymore. But they are brilliant here, adding acidity and sweet nuttiness to this winter salad.

01 Build the salads. Peel away the large outer chicory leaves and divide them between four plates. Slice the chicory hearts up and divide between plates. Halve the apples, remove the cores, cut into slices and place on top of the chicory. Open and drain the packs of beetroot, cut into wedges and scatter over each plate.

02 Use a fork to get the pickled walnuts out of the jar. Roughly chop, then sprinkle them on top of the salads. Crumble the blue cheese directly over each salad.

03 Drizzle each plate with a generous glug of extra virgin olive oil and then spoon over some of the pickling juice from the walnut jar. Season with salt and black pepper. Tear the crusty baguette into four portions and serve on the side.

SPEED HACK
Build the salad straight onto plates. Use the liquid from the pickled walnuts as the acid element in your dressing.

MOB Time:
11 mins, 55 secs

Hablot Brown
Peace of Mind

SERVES 4

HALLOUMI FATTOUSH SALAD

We are massive fans of the fattoush and with this version, adding fried halloumi and za'atar (a Middle Eastern sesame, thyme and spice blend), we've outdone ourselves. Try it – thank us later.

INGREDIENTS
4 pitta breads
6 large vine tomatoes
1 cucumber
2 baby gem lettuces
4 spring onions (scallions)
1 large bunch fresh parsley
1 small bunch fresh mint
1 lemon
2 tbsp za'atar
2 x 225-g (8-oz) blocks of halloumi (check the label if cooking veggie and find an alternative if needed)
extra virgin olive oil
salt and black pepper

GET READY
sharp knife
chopping board
your largest serving bowl
tablespoon
large frying pan (skillet)
scissors
fish slice/spatula
4 serving plates

01 Toast the pitta breads, turning them so that they get crisp on both ends. Set aside.

02 Meanwhile, roughly chop the tomatoes and scrape into your largest serving bowl. Cut the cucumber into half-moons, slice up the baby gem and spring onions and pile them all on top of the tomatoes. Roughly chop the parsley (stalks and all) and scrape into the salad bowl. Pick the mint leaves (discarding the stalks) and add to the bowl. Cut the lemon in half and squeeze the juice into the salad through your fingers to catch any pips. Add 1 tablespoon of the za'atar and season with salt and black pepper.

03 Get a large frying pan over a high heat. Cut both blocks of halloumi into slices. Drizzle a splash of extra virgin olive oil into the pan, then add the halloumi slices. Fry for 2 minutes on one side.

04 Meanwhile, snip the toasted pittas into rough croutons straight into the salad bowl. Drizzle in a good glug of extra virgin olive oil. Give the salad a good toss with your hands.

05 Back to the halloumi. Turn and sprinkle over the remaining 1 tablespoon of za'atar. Fry for a further minute until the underside is crisp. Top the fattoush salad with the fried halloumi and serve at the table for people to help themselves.

SPEED HACK
Pay attention to how we deal with the veg in this recipe. There are a few things to cut and we've chosen the quickest ways to do so.

MOB Time:
11 mins 49 secs

Franc Moody
Dance Moves

V

SERVES 4

MOB FAVOURITE

AVOCADO, KALE & FETA SALAD

INGREDIENTS

2 avocados

2 large lemons

1 tsp ground coriander

dried chilli flakes (hot red pepper flakes)

200 g (7 oz) kale

100 g (3½ oz) mixed seeds

2 yellow (bell) peppers

200 g (7 oz) radishes

200-g (7-oz) block of feta (check the label if cooking veggie and find an alternative if needed)

extra virgin olive oil

salt and black pepper

GET READY

sharp knife

chopping board

spoon

mini food processor

teaspoon

large serving bowl

frying pan (skillet)

4 serving plates

The crunchiness of the raw kale is softened by a creamy spiced lemon and avocado dressing. Salty feta, fresh radishes, sweet pepper and toasted seeds take this kale salad to the next level. Anything but boring.

01 Cut one avocado in half, remove the pit and scoop out the flesh into a mini food processor. Cut the lemons in half and squeeze all the juice into the food processor. Add the ground coriander, a generous pinch of salt, some black pepper, a glug of extra virgin olive oil and chilli flakes to taste. Blitz to a dressing.

02 Tip the dressing into a large serving bowl. Add the bag of kale. Use your hands to massage the dressing into the kale. Set aside.

03 Halve, pit, peel and slice the remaining avocado. Pile on top of the salad. Do not mix.

04 Get a dry frying pan over a medium heat and add the mixed seeds. Let the seeds toast while you deseed and roughly chop the yellow peppers and chop the radishes. Tip the veg and toasted seeds into the salad.

05 Crumble over the feta and give everything a toss to combine. Adjust the seasoning to taste, then serve the salad at the table for people to help themselves.

SPEED HACK

Make the avocado dressing in a food processor. It's quick, super easy and it gives the kale more time in the dressing.

Rita Lee
Lança Perfume

SERVES 4

CHORIZO, WATERMELON & FETA SALAD

INGREDIENTS
2 x 225-g (8-oz) chorizo rings
1 small watermelon
1 bunch fresh mint
4 tbsp sherry vinegar
100 g (3½ oz) blanched
  almonds
200-g (7-oz) block of feta
olive bread
olive oil
salt and black pepper

GET READY
sharp knife
chopping board
large frying pan (skillet)
tongs
4 serving plates
tablespoon
small bowl

A meaty update on the classic watermelon, feta and mint salad. The crispy chorizo and toasted almonds make this a more substantial meal. All that delicious chorizo oil, released while frying, is used here to make the best dressing.

01 Peel the chorizo rings and cut the meat into long diagonal slices. Get a large frying pan over a high heat and drizzle in some olive oil. Place the chorizo slices in a single layer in the pan. Fry for 5 minutes, turning over halfway with tongs, until crisp on both sides and the slices have released their oil.

02 Meanwhile, remove the skin and any visible seeds from the watermelon, chop the flesh into random wedges and divide between four plates. Pick the mint leaves from the mint sprigs and discard the stalks. Set aside.

03 Back to the chorizo. Measure the sherry vinegar into a small bowl, then carefully tip into the pan – stand back as it may catch on fire briefly. Shake the pan a little and then cook for 30 seconds. Spoon the chorizo slices and oily vinegary dressing from the pan on top of the watermelon on each plate.

04 Put the pan back over the heat, add the blanched almonds and fry for 1–2 minutes, stirring, until golden. While the almonds are frying, crumble the feta over the salads and season with salt and black pepper.

05 When the almonds are toasted, tip them over the salads. Scatter over the mint leaves and serve the salads with olive bread.

SPEED HACK
Get the chorizo on to fry as you prep the watermelon. Put every component, as it is ready, onto plates.

Project Pablo
Closer

V

SERVES 4

BREADED GOAT'S CHEESE SALAD

Fried cheese on a salad – a match made in culinary heaven. Creamy melting goat's cheese with chilli jam, olives and sun-dried tomatoes. It's an absolute worldie.

INGREDIENTS
2 x 125-g (4½-oz) hard goat's cheese logs (check the label if cooking veggie and find an alternative if needed)
1 packet of panko breadcrumbs
1 large bag of rocket (arugula)
1 cucumber
1 pot of pitted fresh olives (we like garlic and herb flavoured)
1 pot of fresh sun-dried tomatoes
balsamic vinegar
chilli jam
olive oil
salt and black pepper

GET READY
sharp knife
chopping board
large frying pan (skillet)
fish slice/spatula
large serving bowl
spoon
5 serving plates

01   Cut the rind off the goat's cheese logs, then slice each log into six rounds. Tip the panko breadcrumbs out onto a plate.

02   Get a large frying pan over a medium heat and drizzle in a good glug of olive oil. One by one, put each goat's cheese round onto the plate of breadcrumbs and use your hands to firmly press the breadcrumbs into the cheese to coat on all sides before placing into the frying pan. Fry for 1–2 minutes on each side until golden and oozing.

03   Meanwhile, start to build the salad. Pile the rocket into a large serving bowl. Cut the cucumber into half-moons. Scatter the cucumber, olives and sun-dried tomatoes over the rocket, then drizzle over some oil and balsamic vinegar.

04   Place the fried goat's cheese rounds on top of the salad. Season with salt and pepper and spoon over blobs of chilli jam to serve.

SPEED HACK
Start to assemble the salad while the cheese is frying. Aside from chopping the cucumber, it's a "get everything straight out the pot and throw it in a bowl" kind of job.

MOB Time:
11 mins, 06 secs

Bare Jams
Fishbowl

SERVES 4

SUN-DRIED TOMATO & HERBY YOGURT LENTIL BOWLS

The herby yogurt dressing and salted cashews make these lentil bowls feel a likkle bit naughty. It's the perfect thing to make when you've got the MOB over and you are trying to be healthy.

INGREDIENTS

4 UK medium (US large) eggs
1 small garlic clove
1 small bunch fresh parsley
1 small bunch fresh basil
6 tbsp Greek yogurt
2 pots of sun-dried tomatoes
1 small bag of spinach
3 x 250-g (9-oz) pouches of
   pre-cooked Puy lentils
1 lemon
handful of roasted and salted
   cashews
salt and black pepper

GET READY

boil the kettle
saucepan
mini food processor
tablespoon
large frying pan (skillet)
wooden spoon
sieve
sharp knife
chopping board
4 serving bowls

01 Pour the boiling water from the kettle into a saucepan over a medium heat and bring back to the boil. Add the eggs and set a timer for 6½ minutes (for soft-boiled).

02 Meanwhile, put the garlic clove and most of the parsley and basil, stalks and all, into a mini food processor. Blitz until finely chopped. Add the yogurt and blitz briefly to combine. Season the yogurt with salt and black pepper to taste.

03 Get a large frying pan over a high heat. Tip in the sun-dried tomatoes with their oil and the bag of spinach. Squeeze the unopened lentil pouches with your hands to break up the lentils, then open and tip them into the pan. Add a splash of hot water from the kettle. Season with salt and black pepper, stir and leave to heat through.

04 Drain the eggs into a sieve when cooked and run under cold water until cool enough to handle, then peel and halve. Cut the lemon into four wedges and roughly chop the cashews.

05 Spoon the lentils into four bowls. Drizzle over the herby yogurt, then top each bowl with a halved soft-boiled egg. Tear over the remaining herbs and scatter over the chopped cashews. Season with salt and black pepper and serve with the lemon wedges.

SPEED HACK

Shop-bought shortcuts. Sun-dried tomatoes come in their own oil, so use it to fry the spinach. Ready-roasted cashews mean you don't have to toast them, and a pouch of pre-cooked lentils just needs a little reheat.

MOB Time:
11 mins, 43 secs

Songhoy Blues
Sekou Oumarou

VG

SERVES 4

HARISSA COURGETTE GRAIN SALAD WITH TAHINI DRESSING

This one-pan, creamy spiced grain bowl, which also happens to be vegan, is going to become your Monday night regular. A casual little freshie.

INGREDIENTS

500 g (1 lb 2 oz) courgettes (zucchini)
1 lemon
3 garlic cloves
4 tbsp tahini
2–3 tbsp harissa paste, plus extra to serve if you like
3 x 250-g (9-oz) pouches of pre-cooked mixed grains
1 bunch fresh dill
olive oil
salt and black pepper

GET READY

sharp knife
chopping board
large frying pan (skillet)
garlic crusher
wooden spoon
tablespoon
small bowl
spoon
large serving dish
4 serving bowls

01 Thinly slice the courgettes into half-moon shapes. Cut the lemon in half.

02 Get a frying pan over a high heat and drizzle in a good glug of olive oil. Chuck in the courgettes. Crush in the unpeeled garlic cloves. Fry, stirring occasionally, for 5 minutes until the courgettes are softened and slightly charred.

03 Meanwhile, put the tahini in a small bowl and squeeze in the juice from the lemon halves. Stir, then slowly mix in enough warm water to make the dressing a thick drizzling consistency. (Adding the lemon juice may make the tahini seize up at first, but when you add the water it will turn smooth.) Season with salt and pepper.

04 Back to the courgettes. Add the harissa paste to taste. Squeeze the unopened grain pouches with your hands to break up the grains, then open and tip them into the pan along with a splash of water. Stir and leave to heat through while you chop the dill.

05 Stir the chopped dill through the grain mixture, season to taste with salt and pepper and pile onto a large serving dish. Drizzle over the tahini dressing and serve with extra harissa, if you like.

SPEED HACK
Make the tahini dressing while the courgettes are frying so that they have time to get nicely charred, and crush the garlic cloves into the pan with their skins on.

MOB Time:
11 mins, 23 secs

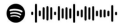

Tinariwen
Sastanàqqàm

V

SERVES 4

GRILLED BROCCOLI, FETA & CHIMICHURRI GRAIN BOWL

INGREDIENTS

400 g (14 oz) Tenderstem broccoli
150 ml (5 fl oz) extra virgin olive oil, plus a splash
1 green chilli
2 garlic cloves
2 small bunches fresh coriander (cilantro)
2 tsp dried oregano
2–3 tbsp red wine vinegar
3 x 250-g (9-oz) pouches of pre-cooked mixed grains
200-g (7-oz) block of feta (check the label if cooking veggie and find an alternative if needed)
salt and black pepper

GET READY

preheat the grill (broiler) to maximum
sharp knife
chopping board
baking tray
tongs
mini food processor
teaspoon and tablespoon
large serving dish
4 serving bowls

Chimichurri is a herby Argentinian sauce usually paired with steak. We've gone veggie here because its chilli heat and acidity also work perfectly with gnarly charred Tenderstem, nutty grains and salty feta.

01 Bunch the broccoli stalks together and chop in half widthways all at once. Lay out in a single layer on a baking tray, drizzle with a splash of extra virgin olive oil and season with salt and black pepper. Grill for 3–4 minutes on each side, turning with tongs, until the broccoli is charred and the stalks are tender.

02 Meanwhile, chop the chilli into quarters and peel the garlic cloves. Put the coriander, stalks and all, garlic and chilli into a mini food processor. Blitz until finely chopped – you may have to unpick the coriander stalks from the blade at first, but persist, they will break down. Once chopped, add the oregano and extra virgin olive oil. Blitz again, season with the red wine vinegar and salt and black pepper to taste.

03 Squeeze the grain pouches to slightly break up the grains, then heat in the microwave following the packet instructions and tip into a large serving dish. Drizzle over most of the chimichurri, then crumble over half the feta and stir together. Top with the charred broccoli and crumble over the remaining feta. Drizzle with extra chimichurri and serve.

SPEED HACK
Whack the grill on before you do anything else. Get a whole bunch of broccoli and cut it all in half at once. Don't worry if the pieces are a bit random, some smaller crispier bits are what you want.

70

SALADS & BOWLS

MOB Time:
12 mins, 00 secs

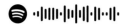

Dominic Fike
Açaí Bowl

V

SERVES 4

GOAT'S CHEESE & PESTO STUFFED PORTOBELLO MUSHROOMS

INGREDIENTS

8 portobello mushrooms
1 tub of fresh basil pesto
  (check the label if cooking
  veggie and find an alternative
  if needed)
2 x 125-g (4½-oz) soft goat's
  cheese logs (again, if cooking
  veggie check the label)
330 g (11½ oz) cherry tomatoes
1 bag of mixed salad leaves
balsamic vinegar
50 g (1¾ oz) pine nuts
olive oil
salt and black pepper

GET READY

preheat the grill (broiler)
  to medium
large baking tray
spoon
sharp knife
chopping board
mixing bowl
4 serving plates
frying pan (skillet)
fish slice/spatula

MOB, you are going to love the contrast here between the fresh balsamic tomato salad and the meaty, cheesy grilled mushrooms with rich nutty pine nuts.

01   Pull out the middle stalk from each mushroom and keep for another time (fry in butter and have with scrambled eggs). Put the mushrooms, hole-side-up, on a large baking tray and dollop a spoonful of pesto into each hole. Cut the goat's cheese logs into four rounds each (to give eight rounds in total) and plonk one round onto each mushroom. Drizzle with olive oil and season with salt and black pepper. Place under the hot grill for 8 minutes.

02   Meanwhile, halve the cherry tomatoes and mix these with the salad leaves in a mixing bowl. Drizzle with a little olive oil and season with salt, pepper and balsamic vinegar to taste. Divide the salad between four plates.

03   Get a frying pan over a medium heat. Add the pine nuts and toast until golden brown, shaking occasionally, then turn off the heat.

04   Use a fish slice or spatula to put two grilled mushrooms on top of each salad and scatter over the toasted pine nuts to serve.

SPEED HACK
Get your mushrooms stuffed and under the grill as fast as you can. Fill the mushrooms with pesto and goat's cheese straight on the baking tray so they are ready to go under the grill.

4

...DS OF EPIC
...VER OPTIONS -
...KEAWAY HEAVEN

RICE &
NOODLES

MOB Time:
11 mins, 23 secs

DJ Yoda
Roxbury

SERVES 4

LA SOBA NOODLES

INGREDIENTS
2 limes
thumb-sized piece of ginger
2 tbsp white miso paste
2 tbsp sesame oil
250-g (9-oz) pack of dried soba
  noodles
200 g (7 oz) radishes
2 avocados
250 g (9 oz) frozen podded
  edamame beans
100 g (3½ oz) pomegranate
  seeds
1 bunch fresh coriander (cilantro)
salt and black pepper

GET READY
boil the kettle
sharp knife
chopping board
large serving bowl
grater
tablespoon
fork/whisk
saucepan
spoon
colander
4 serving plates

One for the healthy MOB. The miso and ginger dressing should be as zingy as possible. You want it to stand up to the soba noodles. Leftovers are just as good, maybe even better, for lunch the next day.

01 Dressing time. Cut the limes in half and squeeze their juices into a large serving bowl. Finely grate in the ginger, add the miso paste and sesame oil and whisk together. Set aside.

02 Pour the boiling water from the kettle into a saucepan over a medium heat and bring back to the boil. Drop in the soba noodles and set a timer for 3 minutes.

03 While the noodles are cooking, finely slice the radishes. Halve the avocados, remove the pits, scoop out the flesh and slice it up. Season the radishes and avo with a little salt and black pepper.

04 Back to the noodles. Chuck in the edamame beans and cook for 1 minute more. Drain into a colander and rinse both under cold water briefly to cool them down. Drain again, then tip into the large bowl with the dressing. Mix everything together well. Top with the sliced avocado, sliced radishes and pomegranate seeds. Tear over the coriander to finish. Serve at the table for people to help themselves.

SPEED HACK
Finely grate rather than chop the ginger. Make the dressing in a large bowl so you can toss the cooked noodles straight into it.

FRESHEST DISH
IN THE BOOK

MOB Time:
10 mins, 59 secs

Imarhan
Tahabort

VG

SERVES 4

COLD TAKEOUT NOODLES

INGREDIENTS
3 limes
6 tbsp smooth or crunchy
   peanut butter
soy sauce
sweet chilli sauce
2 carrots
1 cucumber
1 bunch fresh mint
1 bunch fresh coriander (cilantro)
handful of roasted and salted
   peanuts
dried chilli flakes (hot red
   pepper flakes)
2 x 300-g (10½-oz) packs of
   straight to wok rice noodles

GET READY
boil the kettle
sharp knife
chopping board
large mixing bowl
tablespoon
fork/whisk
peeler
sieve
4 serving plates

The freshest noods in this book. The peanut butter dressing with sweet chilli, soy and lime is unreal. If you like satay, you'll love this.

01 Dressing time. Cut the limes in half and squeeze their juices into a large mixing bowl. Add the peanut butter, 2 tablespoons of soy sauce, 3 tablespoons of sweet chilli sauce and 6 tablespoons of water; whisk together.

02 Peel the carrots and then peel them into long ribbons (leaving the core to munch on), directly into the bowl of dressing. Slice the cucumber into half-moons and add to the bowl too. Roughly chop the mint, coriander and peanuts. Scrape most of the herbs and peanuts into the bowl. Sprinkle in some chilli flakes.

03 Put the rice noodles in a sieve and pour over boiling water from the kettle over the sink to refresh. Rinse thoroughly under cold water to cool. Shake off any excess water and tip the noodles into the bowl with all the other ingredients. Toss together.

04 Divide the noodles between plates and scatter over the remaining herbs and peanuts. Serve with extra sweet chilli and soy sauce.

SPEED HACK
Make up the dressing in a large mixing bowl, then peel the carrots directly into it and scrape in the chopped herbs and vegetables as and when they are ready. This one-bowl method saves on washing up too.

MOB Time:
10 mins, 23 secs

Hollie Cook
Angel Fire

CHEAT'S DAN DAN NOODLES

SERVES 4

*TAKE A PHOTO AND
SHARE YOUR NOODLES
WITH THE MOB
#FEEDTHEMOB*

INGREDIENTS
6 pork sausages
1 tsp five-spice powder
2 pak choi (bok choy)
2 spring onions (scallions)
2 tbsp tahini
2 tbsp dark soy sauce
2–4 tbsp chilli oil with sediment
   (we used Lee Kum Kee)
2 x 300-g (10½-oz) packs of
   straight to wok udon noodles
neutral oil, such as groundnut
salt and black pepper

GET READY
large frying pan (skillet) or wok
teaspoon
wooden spoon
sharp knife
chopping board
fork
tablespoon
small bowl
tongs
4 serving bowls

If we can implore you to cook one recipe from the book, this is it. Dan Dan noodles are one of our most loved takeouts, and this dish manages to pack that epic flavour punch within a fraction of the time and ingredients. Easy.

01   Get a large frying pan or wok over a high heat. Drizzle in a splash of neutral oil and then squeeze the sausages out of their skins straight into the pan. Add the five-spice powder and some salt and black pepper. Leave to fry for 5 minutes, stirring occasionally to break up the meat, until crisp.

02   Meanwhile, slice the white stalks of the pak choi and separate the leaves but keep them whole. Finely slice the spring onions. Set both aside.

03   Dan Dan sauce time. Use a fork to mix together the tahini, dark soy sauce and as much chilli oil as you can handle with 2 tablespoons of hot water in a small bowl.

04   Back to the sausage meat, add the noodles and pak choi stalks to the pan. Stir-fry, tossing everything together using tongs, for 1 minute, then pour in the Dan Dan sauce along with the pak choi leaves. Stir-fry for a further minute, then top the noodles with the sliced spring onions and divide between four bowls to serve.

SPEED HACK
Five-spice + sausage meat. These two ingredients fried together until crisp is a cheat's way of emulating the traditional Sichuan peppercorn-spiced pork.

MOB Time:
11 mins, 16 secs

Easy Kabaka Brown
Belema

SERVES 4

HOISIN CHICKEN EGG NOODLES

INGREDIENTS

1 large pack of mini chicken
  fillets (approx. 640 g/1 lb 7 oz)
2 tbsp sesame oil
1 large red chilli
100 g (3½ oz) cashews
200 g (7 oz) sugar snap peas
2 x 300-g (10½-oz) packs of
  straight to wok fresh egg
  noodles
6 tbsp hoisin sauce
2 tbsp soy sauce
salt and black pepper

GET READY

large frying pan (skillet) or wok
tablespoon
wooden spoon
sharp knife
chopping board
4 serving bowls

Sticky chicken noodles – it's always going to be a winner. We've added cashews and chilli for some crunchy texture and spice. Feel free to up the amount of raw chilli served on top if you are a heat freak.

01 Get a large frying pan or wok over a high heat. Season the mini chicken fillets with salt and black pepper. Add the sesame oil to the pan, then tip in the chicken. Leave to fry, stirring occasionally, while you thinly slice the red chilli.

02 Back to the chicken. Add three-quarters of the chilli and the cashews. Fry, stirring occasionally, for 5 minutes, then add the sugar snap peas and noodles to the pan.

03 Add the hoisin sauce and soy sauce and toss everything together to coat. Stir-fry for 1 final minute before piling into four bowls. Top with the remaining chilli to serve.

SPEED HACK

Mini chicken fillets. These pre-cut chicken breast fillets are a real time saver. Season with salt and pepper still in the packet, then tip straight into a hot pan.

MOB Time:
9 mins, 55 secs

Lord Echo
Low To The Street

SERVES 4

PIMPED UP PACKET RAMEN

SERVE WITH EXTRA SRIRACHA IF YOU LIKE IT SPICY

INGREDIENTS

280 g (10 oz) firm tofu (we used The Tofoo Co. smoked naked tofu)
2 tbsp sesame oil
4 packs of instant veggie ramen noodles
2 spring onions (scallions)
2 pak choi (bok choy)
1 bunch fresh coriander (cilantro)
hot sauce (we used Sriracha)

GET READY

boil the kettle
sharp knife
chopping board
large frying pan (skillet)
tablespoon
tongs
large saucepan
ladle
4 serving bowls

After a long day, sometimes all you need is some packet ramen. We've pimped it up with some crispy sesame oil fried tofu, spring onions, pak choi and fragrant coriander. All doused in hot sauce, bringing that ultimate comfort kick.

01 Drain the tofu and cut into chunks. Get a large frying pan over a medium heat. Add the sesame oil and tofu and fry for about 5 minutes, turning occasionally with tongs, until golden all over.

02 Meanwhile, pour boiling water from the kettle into a large saucepan over the heat as per the packet ramen instructions. Add the noodles along with their spice sachets. Boil for 2 minutes.

03 While this is happening, thinly slice the spring onions and cut the pak choi into quarters lengthways. Drop the pak choi into the saucepan with the noodles. Cook for 2 minutes more.

04 Ladle the ramen noodles and pak choi between four bowls, using the tongs to help pick up the slippery noodles. Top each one with the crispy tofu, scatter over the spring onions, tear over the coriander and serve with hot sauce.

SPEED HACK

Cook the pak choi with the noodles in the packet ramen broth. Use both tongs and a ladle to divide between bowls.

Ekkah
Backseat Driver

SERVES 4

KIMCHI FRIED RICE

INGREDIENTS

2 pak choi (bok choy)
sesame oil, for frying
215 g (7½ oz) jarred kimchi
2 x 250-g (9-oz) pouches of
  pre-cooked basmati rice (we
  use Tilda)
4 UK large (US extra-large)
  eggs
2 tbsp mixed black and white
  sesame seeds
1 tsp dried chilli flakes (hot red
  pepper flakes)
1 bunch fresh coriander
  (cilantro)

GET READY

sharp knife
chopping board
2 large frying pans (skillets) or
  one pan and a wok
fork
wooden spoon
tablespoon
teaspoon
4 serving bowls

SUCH A GREAT DISH. ALSO WORKS FOR BRUNCH

Kimchi is king. If cooking veggie, check your kimchi jar to make sure it doesn't contain any shrimp. Otherwise go bold, the more potent the kimchi – the better the rice. Once you've made this, there is no looking back.

01 Slice the pak choi, keeping the white stalks and leaves separate, and set aside.

02 Get a large frying pan or wok over a high heat. Drizzle in some sesame oil and use a fork to add the kimchi straight from the jar, (saving the juice for later) and the white pak choi stalks. Stir-fry for 1 minute, then tip in the pouches of rice. Use the back of your spoon to break up the rice grains and give everything a good stir. Turn down the heat to medium.

03 Get a second large frying pan over a high heat and drizzle in a good glug of sesame oil. Crack in the eggs. Once the whites begin to set, sprinkle over the sesame seeds and chilli flakes, then use a spoon to baste the egg whites with the sesame oil until they begin to crisp. Turn off the heat.

04 Back to the rice. Turn the heat back up and then stir through a large splash of kimchi juice and the pak choi leaves. Tear in most of the coriander leaves. Cook for a further minute.

05 Divide the kimchi fried rice between four bowls. Top each portion with a sesame and chilli fried egg and tear over the remaining coriander leaves to serve.

SPEED HACK
Don't bother chopping the kimchi, get it straight into the pan. Save all the kimchi juices to flavour the dish once all the rice has been mixed in.

MOB Time:
11 mins, 15 secs

Sivuca
Ain't No Sunshine

SERVES 4

CHORIZO CAULIFLOWER FRIED RICE

Sometimes we want a healthier version of our favourite dish. This recipe is for then. Cauliflower 'rice' works perfectly here because it soaks up the flavour from the chorizo, ginger, garlic and soy.

INGREDIENTS
225-g (8-oz) chorizo ring
2 garlic cloves
thumb-sized piece of fresh ginger
1 small pack of mixed baby corn and mangetout (snow peas)
1 medium cauliflower
250 g (9 oz) frozen podded edamame beans
4 UK medium (US large) eggs
3 tbsp soy sauce
handful of fresh coriander (cilantro)
chilli sauce
olive oil

GET READY
sharp knife
chopping board
large frying pan (skillet)
grater
wooden spoon
mini food processor
tablespoon
4 serving bowls

01 Peel the chorizo and cut it into long diagonal slices. Get a large frying pan over a medium heat and drizzle in a little oil. Add the chorizo, then finely grate the garlic and ginger straight into the pan. Chuck in the baby corn and mangetout. Leave to fry for about 5 minutes, stirring occasionally.

02 Meanwhile, roughly chop the cauliflower. Pulse the cauliflower to the texture of 'rice' in a mini food processor, working in batches if you need to – it will only take 30 seconds at a time. Tip the cauliflower rice straight into the frying pan.

03 Turn up the heat. Add the edamame beans and give everything a good mix. Push the contents of the pan to one side and then crack the eggs into the free space. Use the wooden spoon to scramble the eggs together, then stir them into the cauliflower rice. Fry for a further 2 minutes more.

04 Pour in the soy sauce and give everything a final mix. Tear over the coriander and drizzle with chilli sauce. Serve at the table straight from the pan for people to help themselves.

SPEED HACK
Blitz the cauliflower in batches, then tip each batch straight into the frying pan. It is so fine that it cooks in minutes.

MOB Time:
12 mins, 00 secs

Nicola Conte
Kind of Sunshine

SERVES 4

SATAY CHICKEN RICE BOWLS

This recipe epitomizes the challenges we had while writing this book. It took about 15 attempts to get it ready in time without compromising on taste. You're gonna be happy we persisted, because the satay sauce is an absolute banger.

INGREDIENTS
1 large pack of mini chicken fillets
 (approx. 640 g/1 lb 7 oz)
2 limes
4 tbsp smooth or crunchy peanut
 butter
2 tbsp soy sauce, plus extra to serve
50 g (1¾ oz) creamed coconut
 (¼ of a block)
1–2 tsp dried chilli flakes (hot red
 pepper flakes), plus extra to serve
250 g (9 oz) frozen podded
 edamame beans
200 g (7 oz) mangetout (snow peas)
2 x 250-g (9-oz) pouches of
 pre-cooked wholegrain rice
1 small bunch fresh coriander
 (cilantro)
olive oil
salt and black pepper

GET READY
boil the kettle
large frying pan (skillet)
wooden spoon
sharp knife
chopping board
tablespoon and teaspoon
bowl
measuring jug (pitcher)
fork
4 serving bowls

01 Get a large frying pan over a high heat. While it is getting hot, season the mini chicken fillets lightly with salt and black pepper. Drizzle some olive oil into the pan. Chuck in the chicken and fry for 5 minutes, stirring occasionally, until browned.

02 Meanwhile, cut one lime in half and the other into four wedges. Set aside.

03 Satay sauce time. Put the peanut butter, soy sauce, creamed coconut and chilli flakes to taste into a bowl. Squeeze in the juice of the lime halves. Measure out 300 ml (10 fl oz) of boiling water from the kettle and pour into the satay mix. Stir with a fork briefly to combine – don't worry if there are a few lumps of coconut as they will cook out in the pan later.

04 Pour the satay sauce over the chicken in the pan and tip in the edamame beans and mangetout. Tip in the packets of rice, stir to break up the grains, then cook for a further 2 minutes to heat the rice through until steaming.

05 Pile the satay chicken rice into four bowls and then tear over the coriander. Scatter with extra chilli flakes and serve with the lime wedges and extra soy sauce, if you like.

SPEED HACK
Before you do anything else, get your frying pan over the heat. You want it to be nice and hot, so that your chicken browns.

De Frank Professionals
Afe Ato Yen Bio

SERVES 4

PERI PERI CHICKEN & WILD RICE

A HEALTHY TAKE
ON THE CLASSIC

INGREDIENTS
2 knobs (pats) of butter
1 large pack of mini chicken
   fillets (approx. 640 g/1 lb 7 oz)
2 garlic cloves
2 x 250-g (9-oz) pouches of
   pre-cooked wild rice (we use
   Tilda Basmati and Wild Rice)
1 x 198-g (7-oz) tin of sweetcorn
4 handfuls of kale
dried chilli flakes (hot red
   pepper flakes)
4 tbsp peri peri sauce
   (whatever heat you like)
1 lime
1 small bunch fresh coriander
   (cilantro)
olive oil
salt and black pepper

GET READY
2 large frying pans (skillets)
cutlery knife
2 wooden spoons
garlic crusher
tin opener
tablespoon
sharp knife
chopping board
4 serving bowls

Spicy, buttery chicken with the freshest, garlicky sweetcorn, kale and coriander wild rice. If you love a cheeky Nando's, then this one's for you.

01 Get two large frying pans over a high heat and add a knob of butter to each along with a splash of oil. Season the chicken fillets with salt and black pepper and chuck into one of the pans. Fry for 4 minutes, stirring occasionally.

02 Meanwhile, crush the unpeeled garlic cloves into the other pan, stir and cook for 30 seconds. Squeeze the unopened wild rice pouches with your hands to break up the grains, then open and tip the rice into the pan with the garlic. Open and empty in the tin of sweetcorn with its juices and add the kale. Season with salt, pepper and chilli flakes to taste. Leave to heat through.

03 Back to the chicken. Pour in the peri peri sauce and cook, occasionally basting the chicken with the sauce, for 2 more minutes until the chicken is cooked through.

04 Cut the lime into four wedges.

05 Divide the rice between four bowls and top with the peri peri chicken. Add a lime wedge to each bowl and tear over some coriander to serve.

SPEED HACK
Get both frying pans over a high heat at the same time with a knob of butter and a splash of oil in each. That way, once you've started frying the chicken, you are ready to go with the rice.

OYSTER SAUCE STIR-FRIED GREENS

SWITCH OYSTER SAUCE WITH
SWEET CHILLI SAUCE FOR A
NICE VEGAN TAKE

INGREDIENTS

2 pak choi (bok choy)

2 tbsp sesame oil

1 small bag of sugar snap peas

1 small bag of mangetout
(snow peas)

1 small bag of trimmed green
beans

thumb-sized piece of fresh
ginger

3 tbsp oyster sauce

2 tbsp soy sauce

2 x 250-g (9-oz) pouches
of pre-cooked basmati rice

ready-made crispy fried
onions

GET READY

sharp knife

chopping board

large frying pan (skillet)

tablespoon

grater

wooden spoon

4 serving bowls

Oyster sauce isn't an ingredient we've used a lot at MOB, until now. These fresh greens are packed full of its sticky, savoury flavour and served with fluffy basmati rice and crispy fried onions. A total game changer.

01   Cut the pak choi into quarters lengthways.

02   Get a large frying pan over a high heat. Add the sesame oil, sugar snap peas, mangetout, green beans and pak choi. Finely grate the ginger straight into the pan. Give everything a good toss in the oil and fry for 1 minute.

03   Add the oyster sauce, soy sauce and 50 ml/2 fl oz of water. Stir-fry for 1–2 minutes until the greens are just cooked and coated in the sauce.

04   Meanwhile, squeeze the rice pouches to slightly break up the grains, then heat in the microwave following the packet instructions. Divide between four bowls. Top the rice with the stir-fried greens. Scatter over crispy fried onions to serve

SPEED HACK
Finely grate the ginger straight into the pan instead of chopping it. Use ready-made crispy onions to garnish – they are so moreish and a bit naughty.

MOB Time:
10 mins, 00 secs

Fern Kinney
Love Me Tonight (Love, Love, Love)

SERVES 4

PRAWN, COCONUT & SPINACH CURRY

INGREDIENTS
thumb-sized piece of fresh
    ginger
3–4 tbsp Thai red curry paste
330 g (11½ oz) cherry tomatoes
150 g (5½ oz) creamed
    coconut (⅔ of a block)
2 x 165-g (5¾-oz) packs of
    fresh raw peeled king prawns
    (jumbo shrimp)
200 g (7 oz) baby leaf spinach
1 small bag of sugar snap peas
2 x 250-g (9-oz) pouches of
    pre-cooked basmati rice
2 limes
fish sauce
olive oil

GET READY
boil the kettle
large saucepan
grater
tablespoon
wooden spoon
measuring jug (pitcher)
spoon
sharp knife
chopping board
4 serving bowls

The secret to this prawn curry is buying the best Thai red curry paste you can find. You want one that is both punchy and aromatic as it will be cooled by the sweetness of the tomatoes and the creamy coconut milk.

01 Get a large saucepan over a low heat. Drizzle in a good splash of olive oil, then finely grate the ginger directly into the pan. Add the curry paste, according to how spicy you like it, then turn up the heat to high and fry, stirring, for 1 minute to cook out the spices.

02 Chuck in the whole cherry tomatoes and cook for 2 minutes until they begin to burst. Meanwhile, put the creamed coconut in a jug and pour over 500 ml (18 fl oz) boiling water from the kettle. Stir to break the coconut up slightly, then pour into the saucepan.

03 Bring the curry sauce to a rolling boil, then tip in the prawns, spinach and sugar snap peas. Allow the spinach to wilt briefly, then give everything a good mix. Cook for 1–2 minutes until the prawns have just turned pink, then turn off the heat. If the curry sauce looks a little thick, add a splash of water to thin it slightly.

04 Squeeze the rice pouches to slightly break up the grains, then heat in the microwave following the packet instructions. Cut one lime in half and the other into four wedges. Squeeze the juice of the lime halves into the curry and season with fish sauce to taste. Divide the rice between four bowls and spoon over the curry. Serve with the lime wedges for squeezing over.

SPEED HACK
Aside from cutting up two limes, this recipe requires no chopping and only uses one pan. It couldn't be simpler.

PASTA & GNOCCHI

OUR FAVOURITE
CHAPTER -
ENJOY MOB

5

MOB Time:
11 mins, 00 secs

Chaos In The CBD
Midnight in Peckham

SERVES 4

GARLIC, CHILLI & OLIVE OIL LINGUINE

INGREDIENTS
500 g (1 lb 2 oz) dried linguine
  (check the label if cooking
  vegan and find an alternative
  if needed)
4 fat garlic cloves
2 red chillies
1 bunch fresh parsley
1 lemon
olive oil
salt and black pepper

GET READY
boil the kettle
large saucepan
sharp knife
chopping board
large frying pan (skillet)
wooden spoon
tongs
4 serving bowls

Pasta with garlic, chilli and olive oil is an Italian classic. The key to its simplicity is using enough oil to fry the garlic and chilli in so that it absorbs all that flavour. Don't be shy; the oil is the basis of the sauce.

01 Pour the boiling water from the kettle into a large saucepan over the heat and bring back to the boil. Season the water with salt, then drop in the linguine. Cook for 1 minute less than the packet instructions say to.

02 Meanwhile, finely chop the garlic cloves, then finely chop the chillies. Move both to one side of your board and roughly chop the parsley. Cut the lemon in half.

03 Get a large frying pan over a low heat and drizzle in enough olive oil to cover the base. Scrape in the garlic and chilli and cook for 1–2 minutes, stirring, until the garlic is just turning golden, then turn off the heat.

04 Use tongs to transfer your cooked linguine straight to the frying pan. Add the parsley, grind in plenty of black pepper and squeeze in the juice of the lemon halves. Add an extra drizzle of olive oil, toss everything together and then serve into four bowls.

SPEED HACK
Use tongs to add the linguine straight to the oil in the pan. It saves time draining the pasta and means some of the cooking water is transported to create a luscious sauce.

MOB Time:
11 mins, 34 secs

Louie Austen
Myamy

VG

SERVES 4

COURGETTE, GARLIC & BASIL SPAGHETTI

INGREDIENTS
500 g (1 lb 2 oz) dried
   spaghetti (check the label if
   cooking vegan and find an
   alternative if needed)
500 g (1 lb 2 oz) courgettes
   (zucchini)
1 fat garlic clove
2 lemons
1 small bag of rocket (arugula)
dried chilli flakes (hot red
   pepper flakes)
1 bunch fresh basil
extra virgin olive oil
salt and black pepper

YOU WILL NEED
boil the kettle
large saucepan
grater
large bowl
sharp knife
chopping board
large spoon
colander
4 serving bowls

Raw courgette and peppery rocket are combined with garlic, chilli, lemon and olive oil here to create a fresh-tasting meal. Taste your sauce and make sure it's super punchy – think salad dressing vibes – as the flavours will mellow once you've added the spaghetti.

01   Pour the boiling water from the kettle into a large saucepan over the heat and bring back to the boil. Season the water well with salt, then drop in the spaghetti. Cook for 1 minute less than the packet instructions say to.

02   Meanwhile, coarsely grate the courgettes into a large bowl. Finely grate in the garlic clove and lemon zest. Cut the lemons in half, squeeze the juice of one over the courgettes (reserving the other), then drizzle in two generous glugs of extra virgin olive oil. Tip in the rocket and as many chilli flakes as you'd like. Season with a generous amount of salt and black pepper and mix well.

03   Drain the pasta in a colander, then tip back into the saucepan. Scrape in the courgettes with any juices and tear in most of the basil. Give everything a good mix. Taste, adding the juice of the other lemon if you like, then pile into four bowls. Drizzle each portion with some more extra virgin olive oil, then scatter over the remaining basil leaves to serve.

SPEED HACK
Squeeze the lemon juice through your fingers. This way you will catch any pips and won't have to spend time fishing them out.

Baxter Dury
Miami

V

SERVES 4

CAPRESE GNOCCHI

INGREDIENTS

1 red onion
750 g (1 lb 10 oz) cherry
   tomatoes
2 x 500-g (1-lb 2-oz) packets
   of fresh gnocchi
1 bunch fresh basil
1 tbsp red wine vinegar
1–2 tsp dried chilli flakes (hot
   red pepper flakes)
2 x 125-g (4½-oz) mozzarella
   balls (check the label if
   cooking veggie and find an
   alternative if needed)
olive oil
salt and black pepper

GET READY

boil the kettle
large frying pan (skillet)
grater
wooden spoon
large saucepan
sieve/colander
tablespoon
teaspoon
4 serving bowls

We've taken everyone's favourite sally and made it into a gnocchi recipe. What more do you want? This is about as easy as they come, and it will become one of your staples.

01 Get a large frying pan over a medium heat and pour in a good glug of olive oil. Peel the onion and then coarsely grate it straight into the pan. Fry for a minute to soften, then chuck in the cherry tomatoes and stir. Turn the heat up and leave the tomatoes to bubble away, burst and create a sauce.

02 Meanwhile, pour the boiling water from the kettle into a large saucepan over the heat and bring back to the boil. Season well with salt and drop in the gnocchi. Cook for 1–2 minutes. When the gnocchi float to the surface they are done. Drain through a sieve or colander.

03 Back to the sauce. Tear in half the basil leaves, add the red wine vinegar, chilli flakes to taste and salt and black pepper. Tip in the drained gnocchi and give everything a good stir. Drain the mozzarella balls of any liquid, then tear the mozzarella straight into the pan and leave for a minute to melt.

04 Spoon the gnocchi and sauce into four bowls. Tear over the remaining basil leaves and finish with some extra black pepper.

SPEED HACK
Tear the mozzarella straight into the frying pan for pockets of cheese that melt into the tomato sauce.

Sharhabeel Ahmed
Argos Farfish

SERVES 4

ANCHOVY, ASPARAGUS & TOMATO TAGLIATELLE

This is a saucy springtime number. Make sure to transport the tagliatelle with tongs straight to the frying pan, so that you splash in enough pasta water to create the silkiest sauce.

INGREDIENTS

500 g (1 lb 2 oz) dried
   tagliatelle
250 g (9 oz) asparagus
50-g (¾-oz) tin of anchovy
   fillets in oil
3 garlic cloves
330 g (11½ oz) cherry tomatoes
1 small bottle (187 ml/6½ fl oz)
   white wine
Parmesan cheese
1 bunch fresh parsley
olive oil
salt and black pepper

GET READY

boil the kettle
large saucepan
sharp knife
chopping board
large frying pan (skillet)
garlic crusher
wooden spoon
grater
tongs
4 serving bowls

01   Pour the boiling water from the kettle into a large saucepan over the heat and bring back to the boil. Season the water well with salt, then drop in the tagliatelle. Cook for 1 minute less than the packet instructions say to.

02   Meanwhile, snap the woody ends off the asparagus, then cut each spear roughly into 2.5-cm (1-inch) pieces.

03   Get a large frying pan over a high heat and drizzle in a splash of olive oil. Open the tin of anchovies and empty into the pan along with their oil. Crush in the unpeeled garlic cloves. Cook for 1 minute, stirring, until the anchovies have melted.

04   Chuck in the asparagus and whole cherry tomatoes. Fry for 3 minutes, smooshing the tomatoes with the back of your spoon until they have mostly all burst, then pour in the white wine. Let the sauce bubble away until the pasta is ready.

05   While you are waiting, grate a good chunk of Parmesan onto the chopping board.

06   Use tongs to add the tagliatelle straight to the frying pan with the sauce. Add the Parmesan, tear in the parsley, drizzle in some olive oil and season with black pepper. Toss everything together, then pile into four bowls. Serve with more grated Parmesan, obviously.

SPEED HACK

Don't faff around getting the anchovies out of their tin, empty the whole lot with their oil straight into the pan. Use the back of your spoon to smoosh the tomatoes in the pan to create a sauce.

Doctor Rokit
Café de Flore

SERVES 4

BLOODY MARY PENNE

* FOR WHEN YOU'VE GOT SOME LEFTOVER VODKA

INGREDIENTS
500 g (1 lb 2 oz) dried penne
    pasta
knob (pat) of butter
500 g (1 lb 2 oz) passata
    (strained tomatoes)
1 tbsp Worcestershire sauce
3 tbsp vodka
Tabasco
Parmesan cheese (check the
    label if cooking veggie and
    find an alternative if needed)
1 small bunch fresh basil
salt and black pepper

GET READY
boil the kettle
large saucepan
saucepan
tablespoon
wooden spoon
grater
chopping board
colander
4 serving bowls

Ever thought a Bloody Mary would make a banging pasta sauce? Us too, so we chucked it on some penne. Adjust the amount of Tabasco, Worcestershire sauce and black pepper to your taste.

01 Pour the boiling water from the kettle into a large saucepan over the heat and bring back to the boil. Season the water well with salt, then drop in the penne pasta. Cook for 1 minute less than the packet instructions say to.

02 Meanwhile, get another saucepan over a medium heat. Add the butter and let it melt, then pour in the passata. Add the Worcestershire sauce, vodka, a few dashes of Tabasco and season with salt and black pepper to taste. Stir well and leave the sauce to bubble away.

03 While the sauce and pasta are cooking, finely grate some Parmesan cheese onto a chopping board.

04 Drain the cooked penne in a colander and then tip back into the same pan off the heat. Pour the Bloody Mary sauce over the pasta, tear over the basil and give everything a good mix. Pile into four bowls, and top with the grated Parmesan cheese.

SPEED HACK
We use passata rather than chopped fresh tomatoes in this recipe for an immediate Bloody Mary sauce.

MOB Time:
12 mins, 00 secs

Jayda G
Heaven Could Be Lately

SERVES 4

'NDUJA, OLIVE & CAPER SPAGHETTI

INGREDIENTS
500 g (1 lb 2 oz) dried
   spaghetti
1 pot of pitted fresh olives of
   your choice
150 g (5½ oz) 'nduja sausage
   meat
3 garlic cloves
500 g (1 lb 2 oz) passata
   (strained tomatoes)
balsamic vinegar glaze
1–2 tbsp capers
1 small bunch fresh basil
Parmesan cheese
olive oil
salt and black pepper

GET READY
boil the kettle
large saucepan
sharp knife
chopping board
large frying pan (skillet)
wooden spoon
garlic crusher
tablespoon
tongs
4 serving bowls
grater

'Nduja + olives + capers = all the good stuff. This spaghetti is seriously good. One to impress the MOB, they'll think you're Gordon Ramsay.

01   Pour the boiling water from the kettle into a large saucepan over the heat and bring back to the boil. Season the water well with salt, then drop in the spaghetti. Cook for 1 minute less than the packet instructions say to.

02   Meanwhile, roughly chop the olives. Get a large frying pan over a high heat and drizzle in a good glug of olive oil. Add the 'nduja to the pan and fry, smooshing with the back of your spoon to break it up, for 1–2 minutes. Crush in the unpeeled garlic cloves and cook, stirring, for a minute more.

03   Pour in the passata and a splash of balsamic vinegar glaze. Season with salt and black pepper. Bring to the boil, then scrape in the chopped olives and add the capers. Let the sauce bubble away until the pasta is ready. Try the sauce, adding more balsamic and/or seasoning to taste.

04   Use tongs to transfer the spaghetti straight from the saucepan to the frying pan. Toss everything together, then divide between four bowls. Tear over the basil and serve with a hunk of Parmesan on the side ready for grating over.

SPEED HACK
Save minutes on chopping and instead crush the unpeeled garlic cloves straight into the pan with the 'nduja.

MOB Time:
11 mins, 42 secs

Peggy Gou
Starry Night

SERVES 4

PANCETTA, PEA & CAPER ORZOTTO

INGREDIENTS

300 g (10½ oz) dried orzo
   pasta
160-g (5¾-oz) pack of diced
   pancetta
2 garlic cloves
400 g (14 oz) frozen peas
3–4 tbsp capers
300-ml (10-fl oz) pot of crème
   fraîche
1 lemon
Parmesan cheese
olive oil
salt and black pepper

GET READY

boil the kettle
large saucepan
sieve
large frying pan (skillet)
wooden spoon
garlic crusher
tablespoon
grater
4 serving bowls

Presenting, the 'orzotto'. A creamy, tangy, cheesy risotto made out of orzo pasta – what could be better? Make sure to turn down the heat on the frying pan when you add the crème fraîche so it doesn't split.

01 Pour the boiling water from the kettle into a large saucepan over the heat and bring back to the boil. Season the water well with salt, then drop in the orzo pasta. Cook for 1 minute less than the packet instructions say to. Drain in a sieve.

02 Meanwhile, get a large frying pan over a super high heat and drizzle in a splash of olive oil. Add the pancetta and fry, stirring regularly, for about 5 minutes until crisp.

03 Crush in the unpeeled garlic cloves and tip in the frozen peas. Once the peas have begun to defrost and turn bright green, turn the heat down to low-medium. Add the capers and crème fraîche, then give everything a good mix. Finely grate in the lemon zest and season with salt and plenty of black pepper.

04 Tip the drained orzo into the frying pan and mix well, then grate in a good chunk of Parmesan cheese. Stir the Parmesan into the orzo and let it melt to create a silky-smooth risotto vibe. Serve at the table for people to help themselves.

SPEED HACK
Fry the pre-diced pancetta, stirring regularly, over a super high heat to crisp it up, then crush in the unpeeled garlic cloves. No chopping needed.

MOB Time:
10 mins, 21 secs

The Bahama Soul Club
No Words

SERVES 4

CREAMY PANCETTA & FENNEL GNOCCHI

INGREDIENTS
1 large fennel bulb
1 lemon
160-g (5¾-oz) pack of diced
  pancetta
2 x 500-g (1 lb 2-oz) packs
  of fresh gnocchi
2 garlic cloves
2 tsp fennel seeds
300-ml (10-fl oz) pot of crème
  fraîche
Gruyère cheese
olive oil
salt and black pepper

GET READY
boil the kettle
sharp knife
chopping board
large frying pan (skillet)
wooden spoon
large saucepan
sieve/colander
garlic crusher
teaspoon
spoon
grater
4 serving bowls

If you are unsure whether you are a lover of fennel, this is the recipe to convince you. Crispy pancetta, shedloads of grated Gruyère and tangy crème fraîche work together to create this world-beating little number.

01 Cut the root and top off the fennel bulb, discard these but save and chop the fronds. Cut the bulb into quarters lengthways, then slice the quarters into long strips. Cut the lemon in half.

02 Get a large frying pan over a high heat and drizzle in a splash of olive oil. Add the pancetta and sliced fennel. Fry for 5 minutes, stirring occasionally, until the fennel has softened and the pancetta is crisp.

03 Meanwhile, pour the boiling water into a large saucepan over the heat and bring back to the boil. Season the water well with salt and drop in the gnocchi. Cook for 1–2 minutes. When the gnocchi float to the surface they are done. Drain in a sieve or colander.

04 Back to the pancetta and fennel. Crush the unpeeled garlic cloves into the pan and add the fennel seeds and fronds. Stir and cook for 1 minute more, then tip the cooked gnocchi into the pan.

05 Turn the heat down. Spoon in the crème fraîche, then grate some Gruyère cheese straight into the pan. Give everything a good mix to combine and add a splash of water to loosen if the sauce is a bit thick. Season with salt, black pepper and lemon juice to taste. Pile into four bowls to serve.

SPEED HACK
Fry the pancetta with the fennel. The pancetta will crisp as the fennel softens and it has the added bonus of seasoning and flavouring the fennel as it cooks.

Folamour
Night of Desirable Objects

SERVES 4

SICILIAN-STYLE PASTA

This is a flavour bomb. You've got anchovies, capers, garlic, chilli flakes, pine nuts and Parmesan – so much toasty savouriness. And then, when you thought it couldn't get any better, some lightly pickled raisins. Their sweetness brings the kick.

INGREDIENTS
500 g (1 lb 2 oz) dried orecchiette pasta (or small shells if you can't find it)
4 tbsp raisins
1 tbsp red wine vinegar
50-g (¾-oz) tin of anchovy fillets in oil
3 garlic cloves
50 g (1¾ oz) pine nuts
1–2 tbsp capers
1 tsp dried chilli flakes (hot red pepper flakes)
Parmesan cheese
olive oil
salt

GET READY
boil the kettle
large saucepan
tablespoon
small mixing bowl
large frying pan (skillet)
tin opener
garlic crusher
wooden spoon
teaspoon
mug
sieve/colander
grater
4 serving bowls

01 Pour the boiling water from the kettle into a large saucepan over the heat and bring back to the boil. Season the water well with salt, then drop in the orecchiette (or pasta shells). Cook for 1 minute less than the packet instructions say to.

02 Meanwhile, put the raisins into a small mixing bowl, add the red wine vinegar and 2 tablespoons of warm water. Mix together and leave to soak.

03 Get a large frying pan over a medium heat and drizzle in a splash of olive oil. Empty the tins of anchovy fillets, along with their oil, into the pan. Crush in the unpeeled garlic cloves. Cook for 1 minute, stirring, until the anchovies have melted, then tip in the pine nuts. Cook for 1–2 minutes, stirring, letting the pine nuts toast in the pan. Add the capers to taste, chilli flakes and soaked raisins along with their soaking liquid.

04 When the pasta is cooked, save a quarter of a mugful of the cooking water, then drain the rest in a sieve or colander. Tip the pasta into the frying pan with the reserved pasta water. Mix well, then grate in a good chunk of Parmesan and drizzle in a glug of olive oil. Mix again before dividing between four bowls to serve.

SPEED HACK
Toast the pine nuts in with the melted anchovies and garlic, then just add all the other ingredients to the pan to finish making the sauce.

MOB Time:
11 mins, 36 secs

Riccio
Lil Boy

SERVES 4

PARMA HAM CARBONARA

INGREDIENTS
500 g (1 lb 2 oz) dried
  spaghetti
2 packs of Parma ham
2 garlic cloves
6 UK large (US extra-large)
  eggs
200 g (7 oz) Parmesan cheese
olive oil
salt and black pepper

GET READY
boil the kettle
large saucepan
large frying pan (skillet)
wooden spoon
measuring jug (pitcher)
grater
fork
mug
colander
4 serving bowls

A naughty little twist on the carbonara. Made the proper way with NO CREAM, just egg yolks, loads of black pepper and a mound of Parmesan.

01 Pour the boiling water from the kettle into a large saucepan over the heat and bring back to the boil. Season the water well with salt, then drop in the spaghetti. Cook for 1 minute less than the packet instructions say to.

02 Meanwhile, get a large frying pan over a high heat and drizzle in a little olive oil. Tear the Parma ham into small pieces straight into the pan. Bash the unpeeled garlic cloves with the palm of your hand and add to the pan. Stir and fry the Parma ham for about 5 minutes until crisp, then turn off the heat and remove and discard the garlic cloves.

03 Separate the eggs, placing the yolks together in a measuring jug (discard or keep the whites to use for something else). Coarsely grate three-quarters of the Parmesan cheese into the jug and add plenty of black pepper. Lightly whisk together with a fork.

04 When the spaghetti is cooked, take half a mugful of pasta water out of the saucepan, then drain the rest of the pasta in a colander. Chuck the spaghetti into the still-warm pan with the Parma ham. Add the egg yolk mixture and reserved pasta water. Toss everything together well so that each strand of spaghetti is covered in creamy sauce. Pile into four bowls and serve with more black pepper and the remaining Parmesan grated over.

SPEED HACK
Tear the Parma ham into small pieces with your hands straight into the pan. No chopping required.

MOB Time:
12 mins, 00 secs

Orlando Julius
Disco Hi Life

SERVES 4

SPAGHETTI VONGOLE

*A MOB CLASSIC.
GREAT DATE NIGHT
OPTION*

INGREDIENTS
500 g (1 lb 2 oz) dried
  spaghetti
3 garlic cloves
1 bunch fresh parsley
2 tsp dried chilli flakes
  (hot red pepper flakes)
330 g (11½ oz) cherry tomatoes
500 g (1 lb 2 oz) fresh clams,
  cleaned
1 small bottle (187 ml/6½ fl oz)
  white wine
olive oil
salt

GET READY
boil the kettle
2 large saucepans,
  one with a lid
sharp knife
chopping board
teaspoon
wooden spoon
tongs
4 serving bowls

One to impress. Making spaghetti vongole is the best way to say you love someone. Get the best quality clams you can afford as their sweetness will take this up a level.

01   Pour the boiling water from the kettle into a large saucepan over the heat and bring back to the boil. Season the water well with salt, then drop in the spaghetti and cook for 1 minute less than the packet instructions say to.

02   Meanwhile, slice the garlic cloves. Separate the parsley stalks and leaves, slice the stalks and set the leaves aside. Put another large saucepan over a super high heat and splash in a good glug of olive oil. Add the chilli flakes and whole cherry tomatoes. Cook for 2 minutes, then stir in the sliced garlic and parsley stalks and cook for 30 seconds more.

03   Tip in the clams and pour in the white wine. Bring to the boil and then cover with a lid. Cook for 2–3 minutes until all the clams have opened up (get rid of any that haven't). Using tongs, add the cooked spaghetti straight to the saucepan and toss with the clams. Divide between four bowls, tear over the parsley leaves and drizzle over some more olive oil to serve.

SPEED HACK
We use chilli flakes rather than fresh chillies and whole cherry tomatoes chucked into the pan to save time chopping. Make sure that the saucepan for the sauce is over a super high heat so that the tomatoes burst.

FRIDAY NIGHT

PERFECT PRE-WEEKEND RECIPES. GET THE MOB ROUND

6

Red Astaire
Love To Angie

SERVES 4

TIKKA PANEER WRAPS

Say hello papiiii to the ultimate veggie Indian-style kebab. Paneer and peppers are fried in tikka masala curry paste until crisp and served with a speedy raita, roti and mango chutney. Heaven.

INGREDIENTS

2 x 225-g (8-oz) blocks of
   paneer cheese (check the
   label if cooking veggie and
   find an alternative if needed)
3 mixed (bell) peppers
2 tbsp groundnut or sunflower
   oil
3 tbsp tikka masala curry paste
4 tbsp Greek yogurt
handful of fresh mint leaves
½ cucumber
1 fat garlic clove
8 chapattis or rotis
mango chutney
salt and black pepper

GET READY

sharp knife
chopping board
mixing bowl
tablespoon
spatula
large frying pan (skillet)
small serving bowl
grater
4 serving plates

01 Cut each block of paneer into 12 cubes. Deseed and roughly chop the peppers. Scrape both into a mixing bowl. Add the oil and curry paste. Mix to coat the cheese and peppers in the paste.

02 Get a large frying pan over a high heat. Tip in the paneer and peppers along with all the oil and paste. Spread out in the pan and fry for 5 minutes, turning everything regularly with a spatula, until the paneer is crisp on all sides.

03 Meanwhile, make a quick raita. Dollop the yogurt into a small bowl and tear in half the mint leaves. Coarsely grate in the cucumber, then peel and finely grate in the garlic. Season with salt and black pepper and stir.

04 Take the paneer off the heat when ready. Warm the chapattis or rotis in the microwave following the packet instructions and put two on each plate. Spoon over the tikka paneer and peppers, then dollop over some raita and mango chutney. Tear over the remaining mint leaves to finish.

SPEED HACK
Mix the curry paste and oil together in a bowl, then toss all the peppers and paneer in it at the same time for even coverage.

MOB Time:
11 mins, 56 secs

Rick James
Super Freak

SERVES 4

SPICY LAMB HUMMUS BOWL

INGREDIENTS

500 g (1 lb 2 oz) lean minced (ground) lamb
2 (bell) peppers (red, yellow or orange)
1 cucumber
2 tubs of hummus
2 tbsp harissa paste
1 pack of flatbreads
1 pot of pomegranate seeds
small handful of fresh mint
small handful of fresh parsley
olive oil
salt and black pepper

GET READY

large frying pan (skillet)
wooden spoon
sharp knife
chopping board
5 serving plates
spoon
large serving bowl
tablespoon

MOB, once you've made this, you'll never be able to look at your regular hummus snack with the same amount of love again, because you'll know that it needs some crispy lamb on top to make it truly epic.

01 Get a large frying pan over a super high heat and drizzle in a splash of oil. Tip in the minced lamb and use the back of a wooden spoon to break up the meat into small chunks. Fry, stirring occasionally, for about 8 minutes until all the water has evaporated and the mince is getting brown and crisp.

02 Meanwhile, cut and deseed the peppers and cut the cucumber into rough finger-sized crudités and put on a serving plate. Spoon both tubs of hummus into one large serving bowl.

03 Back to the lamb. Add the harissa paste and season with salt and black pepper. Give everything a good mix and then leave to cook for a few minutes more.

04 Toast the flatbreads while you are waiting.

05 Tip the lamb on top of the hummus in the bowl, then scatter over the pomegranate seeds. Tear over the mint and parsley. Serve with the vegetable crudités and toasted flatbreads.

SPEED HACK
Get the pan super hot before adding the lamb. Use your spoon to break up the meat so that it crisps faster. For a vegan take, use Meatless Farm's plant-based Mince – the best in the land.

MOB Time:
11 mins, 35 secs

Average White Band
Pick Up The Pieces

SERVES 4

SURF & TURF FAJITAS

Steak and prawns is a classic combination, and the puurfect filling in our speedy fajitas. Try and get your hands on spicy, rather than smoky, fajita seasoning.

INGREDIENTS

4 spring onions (scallions)
2 (bell) peppers (red, yellow or orange)
250 g (9 oz) baby plum tomatoes
340 g (12 oz) beef medallion steaks
1 packet of spicy fajita seasoning
165-g (5¾-oz) pack of fresh raw peeled king prawns (jumbo shrimp)
8 soft flour tortillas
sour cream
olive oil
salt and black pepper

GET READY

sharp knife
chopping board
large frying pan (skillet)
wooden spoon
4 serving plates

01 Slice the spring onions. Deseed the peppers and cut into strips. Halve the tomatoes.

02 Get a large frying pan over a super high heat and drizzle in a good glug of olive oil. Scrape in all the peppers and half the spring onions and leave to fry for 2–3 minutes until the peppers have softened.

03 Meanwhile, season the steaks on both sides with salt and black pepper and then slice into finger-width strips.

04 Back to the veg. Add the fajita seasoning, give everything a good mix and cook for 1 minute. Chuck in the steak, prawns and tomatoes and cook for 1–2 minutes, stirring occasionally, until the prawns have turned from grey to pink all over. Turn off the heat.

05 Warm the tortillas in the microwave following the packet instructions, then put two on each plate. Top with the surf and turf fajita mix. Scatter with the remaining spring onions and serve with sour cream.

SPEED HACK
As there is no time to make a salsa, chuck the whole plum tomatoes into the frying pan to create an all-in-one fajita package.

SACK OFF YOUR
CHICKEN CLASSIC
+ SWITCH IT UP

MOB Time:
11 mins, 47 secs

Slaves
The Hunter

SERVES 4

SMASHED BROOKLYN BURGERS

This is our freshest burger yet. Use the best quality meat you can afford. Choose mince with a medium-high fat content so that the burgers are extra juicy.

INGREDIENTS

4 burger buns (we like sesame-topped)
2 baby gem lettuces
4 gherkins (pickles)
4 large tomatoes
750 g (1 lb 10 oz) medium-high fat content minced (ground) beef
8 cheese slices
condiments of your choice (we go classic with mayo, ketchup AND mustard)
olive oil
salt and black pepper

GET READY

sharp knife
chopping board
2 large frying pans (skillets)
fish slice/spatula
4 serving plates

01 Cut the burger buns in half. Slice up the baby gem lettuces. Cut each gherkin lengthways into thirds and then slice the tomatoes into rounds. Set all aside.

02 Get two large frying pans over a super high heat for a couple of minutes to make them searingly hot. Divide the minced beef into eight equal portions – don't bother forming them into patties. Drizzle a little oil into each pan, then place four of the beef portions into each pan. Use your fish slice or spatula to smash each one into a thin burger patty shape. (Don't worry about them looking uniform as more craggy edges equals more crispy bits!)

03 Season the top of the meat with salt and black pepper and fry for 2 minutes, undisturbed, then flip. Season the other side of the patties and then place the cheese slices on top. Cook for 1–2 minutes more until the cheese starts to melt.

04 Transfer the burgers from the pans to the plates. Briefly put the buns into the pans over the heat, cut-side down, to toast.

05 Assemble your burgers. Put your condiment of choice on each bottom bun half, followed by a cheeseburger. Top with some lettuce, tomato slices and gherkin slices, then another burger. Finish with more gherkins and sauce and the burger bun lids.

SPEED HACK
Don't form the minced beef into patties. Simply divide the meat into eight portions, then smash each one out into a thin roundish burger shape in the pan.

MOB Time:
11 mins, 30 secs

Danny Brown
Grown Up

SERVES 4

CHORIZO CHILLI STEW WITH GUAC

INGREDIENTS

225-g (8-oz) chorizo ring
450-g (1-lb) jar of roasted red
    (bell) peppers
2 fat garlic cloves
2 tbsp Cajun seasoning
3 x 400-g (14-oz) tins of kidney
    beans
680-g (1½-lb) jar of passata
    (strained tomatoes)
2 limes
2 avocados
1 small bunch fresh coriander
    (cilantro)
extra mature Cheddar cheese
olive oil
salt and black pepper

GET READY

sharp knife
chopping board
large saucepan
2 forks
garlic crusher
tablespoon
wooden spoon
tin opener
sieve
spoon
small bowl
grater
4 serving plates

The ultimate cheat's chilli lacking none of the flavour and served with zingy guac and Cheddar cheese. As an extra, serve with some tortilla chips for scooping – they bring the crunch.

01 Peel the chorizo and slice into rounds, roughly half a centimetre thick. Get a large saucepan over a high heat. Drizzle in some olive oil, then scrape in the chorizo. Leave to fry.

02 Meanwhile, remove the peppers from the jar with a fork, roughly slice and add them to the pan along with the unpeeled garlic, crushing the cloves into the pan. Add the Cajun seasoning and stir, cooking for a further minute.

03 Open the tins of beans, drain the liquid in a sieve and then add to the pan. Pour in the passata. Season with salt and black pepper and give everything a good mix. Bring the chilli to the boil and let it bubble away while you make the guac.

04 For the guacamole. Cut one lime in half and the other into four wedges. Halve and pit the avocados and scoop out the flesh into a small bowl. Squeeze over the juice from the lime halves, season with salt and black pepper and then smash up with a fork. Guac – done.

05 Tear the coriander over the chilli and serve at the table with the bowl of guac, some Cheddar cheese for topping and the lime wedges for squeezing over.

SPEED HACK
Squeeze the lime juice over the avocados and season before you start to mash them. They will be easier to smash as the lime and salt help to break them down.

MOB Time:
11 mins, 15 secs

DJ Koze
It'll All Be Over

SERVES 4

CRISPY TACO BELL-STYLE NACHOS

ULTIMATE NACHOS

INGREDIENTS

500 g (1 lb 2 oz) lean minced
(ground) beef
1 red onion
4 large handfuls of tortilla
chips
2 baby gem lettuces
330 g (11½ oz) cherry tomatoes
150 g (5½ oz) extra mature
Cheddar cheese
2 limes
3 tbsp Cajun seasoning
sour cream
jarred jalapeños
olive oil
salt and black pepper

GET READY

large frying pan (skillet)
wooden spoon
grater
large serving dish
sharp knife
chopping board
tablespoon
4 serving bowls

Become the nacho master with this naughty little number. The key is to get your frying pan super hot when cooking the beef. Everyone loves the crispy bits.

01   Get a large frying pan over a super high heat. Drizzle in some olive oil, then tip in the beef. Use the back of your wooden spoon to break up the meat into small chunks. Peel the red onion, then coarsely grate it straight into the pan over the heat. Fry, stirring occasionally, until all the liquid has evaporated from the pan.

02   Nacho building time. Pile the tortilla chips in a large serving dish. Slice up the lettuces and put straight on top. Squish the cherry tomatoes between your hands on top of the lettuce. Grate the Cheddar (no need to wash the grater first), cut the limes into wedges and set both aside for a moment.

03   Back to the mince. Add the Cajun seasoning and some salt and black pepper. Give everything a good stir and cook for 2 minutes more or until the beef is crisp before taking off the heat.

04   Top the nachos with the crispy beef. Dollop over some sour cream, add jalapeños to taste, and then scatter over the grated cheese. Serve at the table with the lime wedges for people to help themselves. Nachos – done.

SPEED HACK
Coarsely grate the onion into the frying pan. Build your nachos straight into the serving dish. Smoosh the tomatoes with your hands rather than slicing.

MOB Time:
12 mins, 00 secs

DJ Cam
Bounce

SERVES 4

COD WITH SMOKY RED PEPPER BUTTER BEANS

INGREDIENTS

1 tbsp chipotle paste
250 g (9 oz) cherry tomatoes
1 small bottle (187 ml/6½ fl oz) white wine
450-g (1-lb) jar of roasted red (bell) peppers
3 x 400-g (14-oz) tins of butter (lima) beans
4 skinless cod fillets
1 small bunch fresh parsley
1 lemon
Greek yogurt
crusty bread
olive oil
salt and black pepper

GET READY

large high-sided frying pan or casserole pan with a lid
tablespoon
wooden spoon
fork
tin opener
sieve
sharp knife
chopping board
spoon
4 serving plates

The kind of meal you'd demolish on holiday in an old-school bistro. Get a crusty loaf to eat this with – a baguette would be perfect – in order to mop up all the chipotle tomatoey juices.

01 Get a large, high-sided frying pan or casserole pan over a medium heat and drizzle in a good glug of olive oil. Add the chipotle paste and cook, stirring, for 1 minute.

02 Chuck the whole cherry tomatoes into the pan and pour in the white wine. Remove the peppers from their liquid in the jar with a fork and tear into the pan. Open the tins of butter beans, drain into a sieve and then tip into the pan. Season with salt and black pepper and give everything a good mix.

03 Nestle the cod fillets on top of the stew and season the top of the fish with salt and black pepper. Cover the pan with a lid and cook for 5–6 minutes until the fish becomes white and flaky.

04 Meanwhile, roughly chop the parsley, stalks and all, and cut the lemon into four wedges. Once the fish is cooked all the way through, dollop over spoonfuls of cooling Greek yogurt to taste, scatter over the parsley and lemon wedges. Serve at the table with crusty bread for mopping up the juices.

SPEED HACK
Check this out for time-saving hacks: in this recipe the order in which the ingredients go into the pan means that by the time you've drained the butter beans and added them to the pan, you already have a ready-made sauce. Boom.

FLASHY

7

WHEN YOU
NEED TO
IMPRESS THIS
CHAPTER IS
YOUR GO-TO

MOB Time:
12 mins, 00 secs

Honey Mooncie
Should've Been You

SERVES 4

ASIAN STEAK, WATERMELON & PEANUT SALAD

A true summer banger. Zingy, fresh, a bit salty, sweet and sour with some chilli heat. This sally is a belter, you're gonna love it.

01 Get a large frying pan searing hot – this will take a couple of minutes over a super high heat. Meanwhile, cut the limes in half. Thinly slice the red chilli and roughly chop the peanuts. Scrape the chilli and peanuts into a small mixing bowl and set aside.

02 Season the steaks liberally with black pepper on both sides. Drizzle some oil into the frying pan and, once sizzling, add the steaks. Fry for 2 minutes on each side.

03 Dressing time. Crush the unpeeled garlic clove into a large mixing bowl. Add the fish sauce, soy sauce, light brown sugar and a splash of neutral oil. Squeeze in the juice from the halves of one lime. Whisk together with a fork.

04 Once the steaks are cooked, transfer them to the chopping board and leave to rest while you assemble the salad.

05 Separate the baby gem lettuces into leaves straight into the bowl of salad dressing. Toss together, then tip out onto a large platter. Scatter over the watermelon chunks.

06 Thinly slice the steaks, then lay the slices over the salad. Squeeze over the juice of the remaining lime halves. Scatter over the chopped chilli and peanuts to finish. Serve at the table and let people help themselves.

SPEED HACK
Get the frying pan searingly hot before you add the steaks, that way they will caramelize without overcooking.

INGREDIENTS
2 limes
1 red chilli
large handful of roasted salted
  peanuts
340 g (12 oz) beef medallion
  steaks
1 fat garlic clove
2 tbsp fish sauce
1 tbsp soy sauce
1 tbsp light brown soft sugar
3 baby gem lettuces
2 x 400-g (14-oz) packs of
  prepared watermelon chunks
neutral oil, such as groundnut
black pepper

GET READY
large frying pan (skillet)
sharp knife
chopping board
small mixing bowl
tongs
garlic crusher
large mixing bowl
tablespoon
fork
large serving dish
4 serving plates

The Jeremy Spencer Band
Cool Breeze

SERVES 4

ROMESCO GAZPACHO WITH CRISPY 'NDUJA

INGREDIENTS
130 g (4½ oz) smoked almonds
2 x 450-g (1-lb) jars of roasted
   red (bell) peppers
2 tsp smoked paprika
2 tbsp sherry vinegar
100 g (3½ oz) 'nduja sausage
   meat
large handful of ice
small handful of fresh parsley
olive oil
salt and black pepper

GET READY
mini food processor with stick
   blender attachment
large mixing bowl
fork
teaspoon
tablespoon
large frying pan (skillet)
wooden spoon
measuring jug (pitcher)
ladle
4 serving bowls

We are big fans of a romesco – the addictive sauce made from almonds and roasted red peppers. And we've now taken it to another level with this epic gazpacho using smoked almonds and a crispy 'nduja topping. So cooling, so fresh. Go on.

01 Put the almonds into a mini food processor and blitz until very finely chopped, then tip into a large mixing bowl. Remove the peppers from their liquid from one jar using a fork and add to the food processor. Blitz to a purée and then tip into the bowl with the almonds. Repeat with the other jar of peppers. Stir in the smoked paprika and sherry vinegar and add some salt and black pepper to season. Set aside.

02 Get a large frying pan over a high heat and drizzle in some olive oil. Add the 'nduja sausage meat, break it up into small pieces with your wooden spoon and fry for 1 minute until crisp. Turn off the heat and set aside.

03 Fill a measuring jug with 500 ml (18 fl oz) of cold water. Add the ice to the water, then pour into the bowl with the peppers and almonds. Use the stick blender to blitz the contents of the bowl into a fairly smooth gazpacho-style soup.

04 Ladle into four serving bowls, top each one with the crispy 'nduja with its cooking oil and a few parsley sprigs.

SPEED HACK
This is where having a multipurpose food processor really comes into its own. The processor attachment finely chops the peppers and nuts and the stick blender then blitzes the whole soup.

The HU
Wolf Totem

SERVES 4

SEA BASS WITH ORANGE, FENNEL, CHILLI & WATERCRESS

INGREDIENTS

5 tbsp extra virgin olive oil
1½ tbsp sherry vinegar
1 large fennel bulb
1 large orange
1 red chilli
4 skin-on sea bass fillets
1 bag of watercress
50 g (1¾ oz) chopped roasted
    hazelnuts
olive oil
salt and black pepper

GET READY

tablespoon
large bowl
fork
sharp knife
chopping board
large frying pan (skillet)
fish slice/spatula
4 serving plates

This is the perfect recipe for when you want to cook something impressive and healthy. For the crispest sea bass skin, make sure the pan is super super hot before you add the fish, and press down on each fillet with a fish slice or spatula as it is frying.

01 Put the extra virgin olive oil and vinegar into a large bowl, season with salt and black pepper to taste and whisk together with a fork.

02 Cut the root and top off the fennel bulb and discard. Cut the bulb into quarters lengthways, then thinly slice into long strips. Tip the sliced fennel into the bowl with the dressing.

03 Peel the orange, then slice into rounds, removing any big bits of pith and the pips. Add to the bowl with the fennel. Thinly slice the red chilli and scrape into the bowl.

04 Get a large frying pan over a super high heat. Season the sea bass fillets with salt and black pepper on both sides. Once the pan is searing hot, drizzle in a little olive oil and then place the fish fillets in the pan, skin-side down. Press down on each fillet with a fish slice or spatula to encourage them to crisp up evenly. Cook for 2–3 minutes, then flip over and cook for 1 minute on the other side or until the fish is cooked through.

05 While the fish is cooking, tip the watercress and chopped roasted hazelnuts into the bowl with the fennel. Toss everything together with your hands and adjust the seasoning. Divide between four plates. When the sea bass is cooked, serve alongside the salads.

SPEED HACK
Buy ready-roasted chopped hazelnuts. Pre-toasted and pre-chopped = so much time saved.

MOB Time:
11 mins, 47 secs

OOFT!
Love & Soulsaving

SERVES 4

THAI RED MUSSELS

INGREDIENTS

3 tbsp Thai red curry paste
2 x 400-g (14-oz) tins of
  coconut milk
1 kg (2 lb 4 oz) fresh mussels
1 lime
2 spring onions (scallions)
1 small bunch fresh coriander
  (cilantro)
2 x 250-g (9-oz) pouches of
  pre-cooked basmati rice
neutral oil, such as groundnut

GET READY

large saucepan with a lid
tablespoon
tin opener
wooden spoon
large mixing bowl
sharp knife
chopping board
large serving bowl
4 serving bowls

Check over your mussels once you've bought them. If there are any long straggly beards poking out of their shells, pull them out. We've served these mussels with rice to echo the curry vibes, but they would be just as good with some warmed naan bread.

01 Get a large saucepan over a medium heat and drizzle in a good glug of neutral oil. Add the red curry paste and fry to cook out the spices for a minute while you open the tins of coconut milk. Pour the coconut milk into the pan, stir and leave the sauce to bubble away.

02 Half-fill a large mixing bowl with cold water. Empty in the mussels and check over the shells, cleaning them of any grit and pulling out any straggly bits of threads that are poking out (the beards). Discard any mussels that are already open and don't close when you tap them sharply.

03 Drain and discard the water and chuck the mussels into the pan with the coconut milk. Turn the heat up to high, cover the pan with a lid and cook for 3–4 minutes until the mussels have opened (discard any that haven't).

04 Meanwhile, cut the lime into four wedges, slice the spring onions and roughly chop the coriander. Squeeze the rice pouches to separate the grains, then heat in the microwave following the packet instructions.

05 Empty the hot rice into a large serving bowl. Scatter the curry in the pan with the spring onions, coriander and lime wedges for squeezing over. Serve at the table for people to help themselves.

SPEED HACK
Get the sauce made before you tackle prepping the mussels. That way, once you've checked over them, they can be tipped straight into the pan.

MOB Time:
8 mins, 36 secs

Nolan Porter
If I Could Only Be Sure

SERVES 4

GARLIC & CHILLI KING PRAWNS

*TAKE A SNAP AND SHARE YOUR DISH WITH THE MOB #FEEDTHEMOB

The secret to perfect garlic prawns? Butter. Lots of it. This recipe is so simple – it's worth splashing out and buying the best prawns you can get. It might seem gross, but munching on the heads is the best bit.

INGREDIENTS
1 small bunch fresh parsley
1 lemon
1 ciabatta loaf
125 g (4½ oz) butter
3 garlic cloves
1 tsp smoked paprika
dried chilli flakes (hot red
　pepper flakes)
1 kg (2 lb 4 oz) shell-on fresh
　raw king prawns (jumbo
　shrimp)

GET READY
preheat the oven to 180°C fan
　(200°C/400°F/Gas Mark 6)
sharp knife
chopping board
baking tray
large frying pan (skillet)
cutlery knife
garlic crusher
teaspoon
tongs
4 serving plates

01 Roughly chop the parsley and cut the lemon in half. Set both aside to use later.

02 Put the ciabatta loaf onto a baking tray and into the oven to warm through for about 6–8 minutes.

03 Get a large frying pan over a high heat, add the butter and let it melt. Once melted, crush in the unpeeled garlic cloves. Sprinkle in the smoked paprika and as many chilli flakes as you like. Stir, then add the prawns. Fry for 4–5 minutes, turning occasionally with tongs, until the prawns have all turned pink.

04 Take the pan off the heat and squeeze over the juice from the lemon halves. Stir the parsley through and serve with the warmed ciabatta for mopping up the garlic butter.

SPEED HACK
Don't be tempted to continually stir the prawns in the pan. Leave them to go pink on one side before turning. They will cook quicker and absorb more of the banging butter.

MOB Time:
12 mins, 00 secs

Gerry Cinnamon
The Bonny

SERVES 4

SEARED SQUID, CHILLI, TOMATO & CHICKPEA STEW

INGREDIENTS
1 lemon
3 garlic cloves
400 g (14 oz) cherry tomatoes
3 x 400-g (14-oz) tins of
    chickpeas
1 small bottle (187 ml/6½ fl oz)
    red wine
3 tbsp chilli relish or jam, plus
    extra to serve
300 g (10½ oz) prepared fresh
    (or defrosted if fresh not
    available) squid
1 bag of rocket (arugula)
crusty bread
mayonnaise
olive oil
salt and black pepper

GET READY
sharp knife
chopping board
2 large frying pans (skillets)
garlic crusher
wooden spoon
tin opener
tablespoon
tea towel (kitchen cloth)
tongs
4 serving plates

Squid is so tasty when you get it right. Make sure it is COMPLETELY dry before frying and that your pan is screaming hot for the ultimate caramelization. Fried squid on top of a red wine, tomato, chilli and chickpea stew... what more do you want?

01 Cut the lemon into four wedges. Get a large frying pan over a high heat and drizzle in a good glug of olive oil. Crush in the unpeeled garlic cloves and cook for 30 seconds, stirring, then chuck in the whole cherry tomatoes and continue to stir. Open and drain the liquid from the tins of chickpeas and tip them into the pan. Pour in the red wine and add the chilli relish or jam. Season generously with salt and black pepper and leave to bubble away.

02 Get a second large frying pan searingly hot – you want it almost smoking. Meanwhile, pat the squid dry on a clean tea towel, then slice into rings and season with salt and black pepper. Drizzle some olive oil into the very hot frying pan, then tip in the squid. Fry for 2 minutes, moving the squid around the pan with tongs, until it is all evenly charred and tender.

03 Turn off the heat under the chickpea stew and scatter over the rocket, then tip over the charred squid. Serve at the table with lemon wedges, crusty bread, mayo and more chilli relish or jam.

SPEED HACK
We've got two words for you MOB: chilli jam. This hero ingredient adds an instant injection of heat and sweetness which is essential here for mellowing the acidity of the red wine quickly. Get it in your storecupboards and thank us later.

MOB Time:
11 mins, 50 secs

Fort Knox Five
The Brazilian Hipster

SERVES 4

MISO GRILLED SALMON

*THE FLAKIEST
SALMON IN TOWN*

INGREDIENTS
1 bunch spring onions
  (scallions)
3 tbsp white miso paste
1 tbsp soy sauce
1 tbsp sesame oil
1 tbsp rice wine vinegar
1 tsp caster (granulated) sugar
4 skin-on salmon fillets
2 tsp white sesame seeds
1 bunch fresh coriander
  (cilantro)
2 x 250-g (9-oz) pouches
  of pre-cooked basmati rice
neutral oil, such as groundnut

GET READY
preheat the grill (broiler)
  to maximum
baking tray
tablespoon
teaspoon
small mixing bowl
fork or whisk
sharp knife
chopping board
4 serving plates

A MOB favourite. Grilling the spring onions whole reduces waste and is a tasty new way of eating them. The miso sauce is also great with egg fried rice and over roasted aubergine (eggplant).

01 Set one spring onion aside. Place the rest on a baking tray and toss with a little neutral oil. Place under the hot grill for 2 minutes.

02 Meanwhile, it's sauce time. Whisk the miso, soy sauce, sesame oil, rice wine vinegar and sugar together in a small mixing bowl.

03 Remove the tray of spring onions from the grill, place the salmon fillets (we use Alaskan Salmon for its quality and sustainability), skin-side down, on top of the spring onions, then spoon over the miso sauce so that each piece of fish is evenly coated. Place under the grill for 6–8 minutes until the salmon is cooked through and the spring onions are nicely charred. Sprinkle the sesame seeds over the salmon for the final 2 minutes of cooking time.

04 While the salmon is grilling, thinly slice the remaining spring onion and roughly chop the coriander.

05 Squeeze the rice pouches to slightly break up the grains, then heat in the microwave following the packet instructions. Divide the rice between four plates and stir some chopped coriander into each portion. Place a salmon fillet with some charred spring onions onto each plate. Scatter over the sliced raw spring onion to finish.

SPEED HACK
Make sure the grill is hot before you begin so that the spring onions and salmon are grilled in time.

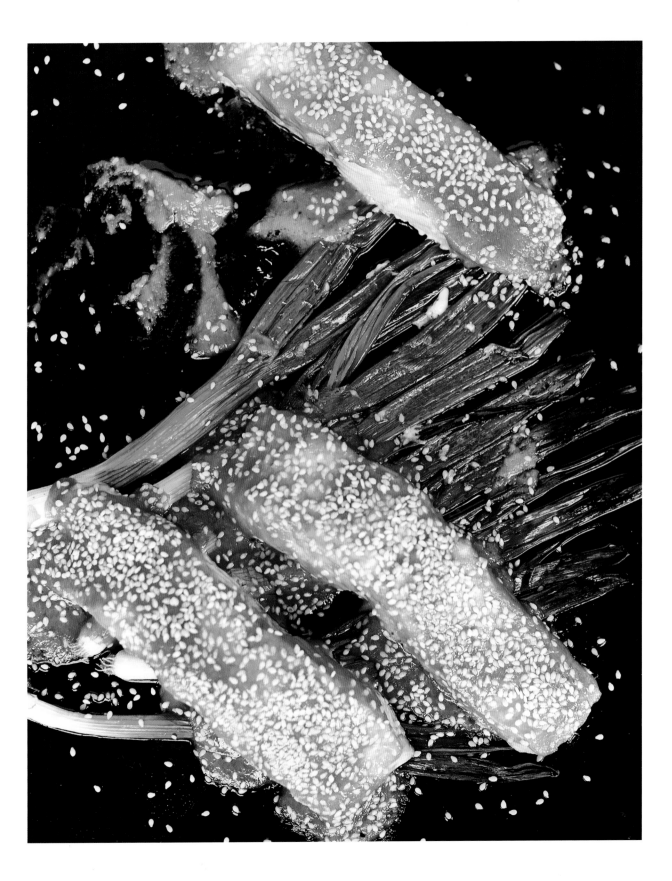

MOB Time:
11 mins, 20 secs

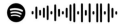

BabeHeaven
Seabird

SERVES 4

CHIPOTLE PRAWNS WITH BUTTERY POLENTA

INGREDIENTS
2 chicken stock (bouillon) pots
   or cubes
butter
2 x 165-g (5¾-oz) packs of
   fresh raw peeled king prawns
   (jumbo shrimp)
1 tbsp chipotle paste
1 x 198-g (7-oz) tin of sweetcorn
200 g (7 oz) quick-cook
   polenta (sometimes called
   pre-cooked)
Parmesan cheese
1 small bunch fresh coriander
   (cilantro)
salt and black pepper

GET READY
boil the kettle
measuring jug (pitcher)
whisk
large saucepan
large frying pan (skillet)
cutlery knife
tablespoon
wooden spoon
tin opener
scales
small bowl
grater
4 serving bowls

If you haven't cooked with polenta before, you're a mug. It is a massively underrated ingredient and it's so good. The quick-cook stuff literally takes a minute to make, has the consistency of proper mash and gets tastier and tastier the more butter and Parmesan you add to it. Ultimate comfort food.

01 Put the chicken stock pots or cubes into a measuring jug, then pour over 1 litre (quart) of boiling water from the kettle and whisk to combine. Pour into a large saucepan and whack over a medium heat to bring back to the boil.

02 Meanwhile, get a large frying pan over a high heat and add a large knob (pat) of butter. Tip in the prawns and chipotle paste and stir. Open and drain the tin of sweetcorn and add to the pan. Fry for 1–2 minutes, stirring occasionally, until the prawns have turned pink all over, then turn the heat down to its lowest setting to just keep the prawns warm.

03 Back to the stock. Weigh out the polenta into a small bowl, then pour it into the boiling stock while whisking constantly to combine. Keep whisking for a minute or so to get out any lumps as the polenta cooks and thickens. Once it's at the consistency of a loose mash, take off the heat, add a big knob of butter and grate in some Parmesan. Season with salt and pepper and stir.

04 Spoon the polenta into four bowls. Top with the chipotle prawns and butter from the pan. Tear over the coriander to serve.

SPEED HACK
Get the chicken stock boiling while you fry the prawns. That way, as soon as they turn pink you can keep them warm while you tip the polenta into the boiling stock, constantly whisking until done.

MOB Time:
12 mins, 00 secs

Action Bronson
Baby Blue

| V |

SERVES 4

BEETROOT SOUP WITH SOUR CREAM & DILL

THE MOST REFRESHING SOUP THIS SIDE OF MOSCOW

INGREDIENTS
2 vegetable stock (bouillon)
   pots or cubes
2 fat garlic cloves
3 x 250-g (9-oz) packs
   of cooked beetroot (not in
   vinegar)
2 tsp cumin seeds
½ cucumber
handful of fresh dill
sour cream
olive oil
salt and black pepper

GET READY
boil the kettle
measuring jug (pitcher)
fork
sharp knife
chopping board
scissors
large saucepan
teaspoon
wooden spoon
stick blender
4 serving bowls

One for the adventurous MOB. This vibrant soup is a banger. The cumin and garlic enhance the beetroot's earthy flavour, while the sour cream, cucumber and dill are fresh counterparts.

01   Put the vegetable stock pots or cubes into a measuring jug. Pour in 1 litre (quart) of boiling water from the kettle. Whisk with a fork to combine and set aside.

02   Peel and slice the garlic cloves. Snip open and drain the beetroot packs and roughly chop. Get a large saucepan over a high heat and drizzle in some olive oil. Add the garlic and cumin seeds and fry for 1 minute, stirring. Add the beetroot to the pan and pour in the stock. Leave to bubble away.

03   Meanwhile, rinse your knife and chopping board. Chop the cucumber into cubes, then roughly chop the dill.

04   Back to the soup. Season with salt and black pepper, then turn off the heat. Use a stick blender to blitz until smooth.

05   Pour the soup into four bowls. Top each one with a dollop of sour cream, a drizzle of olive oil and the cucumber and dill to finish.

SPEED HACK
Ready-cooked beetroot is the hero here. Roughly chop before adding to the pan, the smaller they are the easier it is to blitz.

MOB Time:
11 mins, 17 secs

The Rhythm Method
Party Politics

SERVES 4

PEA & MINT SOUP WITH CRISPY PARMA HAM

Pea and ham is a winning combo. We've given this classic a flashy update by adding some double cream for richness and frying the Parma ham until crisp to sit on top of the soup.

INGREDIENTS
1 fat garlic clove
800 g (1 lb 12 oz) frozen peas
2 tbsp sherry vinegar
2 chicken stock (bouillon) pots
  or cubes
1 small bunch fresh mint
2 packets of Parma ham
150 ml (5 fl oz) double (heavy)
  cream
extra virgin olive oil
salt and black pepper

GET READY
boil the kettle
wide knife
large saucepan
tablespoon
measuring jug (pitcher)
wooden spoon
large frying pan (skillet)
plate
stick blender
4 serving bowls

01 Smash the unpeeled garlic clove with the back of a wide knife and chuck into a large saucepan over a high heat. Tip in the frozen peas, sherry vinegar and chicken stock pots or cubes. Pick the mint leaves and add most of them to the pan (discarding the stalks). Measure out 800 ml (28 fl oz) of boiling water from the kettle and pour in. Stir and season with salt and black pepper to taste. Bring the soup to the boil.

02 Meanwhile, get a large, dry frying pan over a high heat. Add one packet of Parma ham and fry for about 2–3 minutes, stirring, until crisp. Put on a plate and repeat with the remaining packet of ham.

03 Turn off the heat under the soup and remove the garlic clove. Add the double cream and blitz until smooth with a stick blender. Pour into four bowls and top with the crispy Parma ham, remaining mint leaves and a drizzle of extra virgin olive oil.

SPEED HACK
Tip one whole packet of Parma ham into the frying pan at a time over a high heat. The ham will crisp and shrivel into random shapes. It is much quicker than chopping and looks cooler.

SWEET
STUFF

8

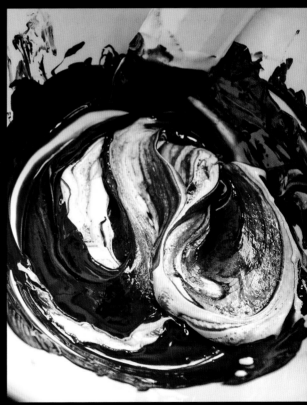

A SELECTION OF
THE SPEEDIEST
DESSERTS FOR THE
SWEET-TOOTHED MOB

MOB Time:
8 mins, 23 secs

Rex Orange County
10/10

V

SERVES 4

CRUNCHY NUT CORNFLAKE CRUMBLE

INGREDIENTS
large knob (pat) of butter
2 large eating apples
500 g (1 lb 2 oz) frozen berries
  of your choice
3–4 tbsp runny honey
2 tsp ground cinnamon
crunchy nut cornflakes
ice cream

GET READY
large frying pan (skillet)
cutlery knife
grater
tablespoon and teaspoon
wooden spoon
4 serving bowls

We are pretty happy with this one. The ultimate cheat's apple and mixed berry crumble made using crushed cereal as the topping. So simple, so effective. It's gonna become a staple.

01   Get a large frying pan over a medium heat and add the butter. Leave to melt while you coarsely grate the unpeeled apples straight into the pan, discarding the cores. Chuck in the frozen berries, add the honey (to your taste) and the cinnamon. Cook, stirring, for 3–4 minutes until the apples and berries have mostly broken down into a compote-like mixture.

02   Spoon the compote into four bowls. Crush a big handful of crunchy nut cornflakes into each bowl over the fruit. Serve with ice cream. Cheat's crumble – done.

SPEED HACK
Make the crumble filling on the hob. Grate the apples straight into the melted butter in a frying pan, then chuck in the pack of frozen berries, cinnamon and honey and cook down.

CRUNCHY NUT
HAS NEVER
BEEN HOTTER

MOB Time:
12 mins, 00 secs

Tom Misch
It Runs Through Me

V

SERVES 4

TWELVE-MINUTE TIRAMISU

INGREDIENTS
2 tbsp instant coffee powder
 or granules
4 tbsp Kaluha or Rum
450 ml (15 fl oz) double (heavy)
 cream
3 tbsp icing (confectioners')
 sugar
1 packet of sponge fingers
cocoa powder

GET READY
boil the kettle
tablespoon
2 mixing bowls
measuring jug (pitcher)
whisk
baking dish
spatula
sieve
4 serving bowls

A tiramisu has got to be up there in our top three desserts. The classic, made with eggs and mascarpone, needs a long time sitting in the fridge before it is ready to eat, which is why here, we have used just pillowy whipped cream with a lot of rum and coffee. Simples.

01 Put the instant coffee into one of the mixing bowls. Measure out 150 ml (5 fl oz) of boiling water from the kettle into a measuring jug. Add to the coffee and stir until dissolved. Add the booze and set aside to cool slightly.

02 Tip the double cream into the other mixing bowl. Add the icing sugar and whisk by hand until the cream just holds its shape – don't overdo it, you want it to be pillowy and light.

03 One by one, dunk half of the sponge fingers into the booze and coffee liquid, for 5–10 seconds at a time (just enough so that they soak up some coffee, but not too long otherwise they will disintegrate) and lay in the baking dish. Spread over half of the whipped cream with a spatula. Repeat the dipping and layering process with the other half of the sponge fingers and cream, making sure that the sponge fingers soak up all the coffee goodness. Pour any extra boozy coffee on top.

04 Sift over some cocoa powder to finish, then dig in. Quickest ever tiramisu – done.

SPEED HACK
Get everything laid out in a production line so that you can dunk the sponge fingers, lay them straight in the dish and then cover in the cream. Having only two layers also helps speed things up.

Loyle Carner
Carluccio

V

SERVES 4

CROISSANT FRENCH TOAST

INGREDIENTS
3 UK medium (US large) eggs
2 tbsp icing (confectioners')
  sugar, plus extra to serve
1 tsp vanilla extract
pinch of salt
100 ml (3½ fl oz) milk
2 knobs (pats) of butter
4 large croissants
flaked (slivered) almonds

GET READY
roasting tin/baking dish
tablespoon
teaspoon
measuring jug (pitcher)
whisk
2 large frying pans (skillets)
cutlery knife
fish slice/spatula
4 serving plates

An almond croissant on acid. It's our favourite type of pud because you could quite easily justify putting it away for breakfast. Be brave when dunking the croissants into the vanilla custard mixture – they can take more than you think.

01 Crack the eggs into a roasting tin/baking dish. Add the icing sugar, vanilla extract and salt. Pour in the milk and whisk to form a custard.

02 Get two large frying pans over a medium heat and put a knob of butter to melt in each.

03 One at a time, dip each croissant into the custard mixture on both sides, squashing it down with a fish slice or spatula so that it soaks up loads of custard. Go bold – the more custard the better. Transfer two custardy croissants to each frying pan.

04 Fry for 1–2 minutes on the first side until deep golden brown. Flip the croissants over and scatter with the flaked almonds. Fry for a further minute until golden on the other side.

05 Transfer the croissants to four plates and dust with more icing sugar to serve.

SPEED HACK
Melt the butter in the frying pans while you are dunking the croissants in the custard mixture. That way they can go straight into the pans to fry.

Al Green
Jesus Is Waiting

VG

SERVES 4

VEGAN CHOCOLATE MOUSSE

THIS NAUGHTY, NAUGHTY LITTLE PUD IS LIFE-CHANGING

INGREDIENTS
200 g (7 oz) vegan dark
   (bittersweet) chocolate, with
   at least 70% cocoa solids
349-g (12-oz) block of silken
   tofu (we use Morinu)
maple syrup
1 tsp vanilla extract
sea salt

GET READY
microwaveable bowl
spoon
mini food processor with stick
   blender attachment
tablespoon
teaspoon
4 serving glasses

Don't tell people this is vegan, and then surprise them...
guaranteed they will never guess that such a rich, silky-smooth
chocolate mousse doesn't contain any eggs or dairy.

01   Snap the chocolate into pieces in its packaging and then empty
into a microwaveable bowl. Blast in the microwave on high for
30 seconds at a time, then stir until all the chocolate has melted.
(Don't cook the chocolate for longer than 30 seconds in one go
as it can burn.)

02   Meanwhile, drain the tofu and put into a mini food processor. Blitz
until really smooth.

03   Scrape the blitzed tofu into the bowl with the melted chocolate.
Add 2 tablespoons of maple syrup and the vanilla extract. Use the
stick blender attachment to blitz the chocolate with the tofu to
create an airy, fluffy mousse-like texture.

04   Spoon the chocolate mousse into four glasses, drizzle with extra
maple syrup if you like and sprinkle with sea salt to serve.

SPEED HACK
Snap the chocolate into rough pieces in its packet and then melt
in the microwave. As long as you keep an eye on it, this is by far
the easiest and quickest way to melt chocolate.

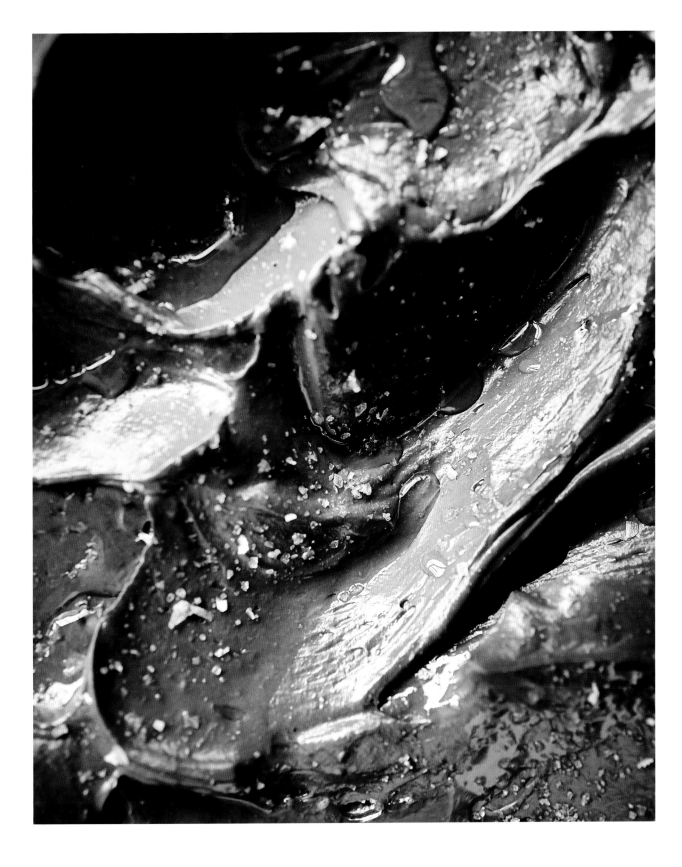

Nina Simone
Don't Let Me Be Misunderstood

VG

SERVES 4

PINEAPPLE WITH CHILLI, SUGAR, SALT & LIME

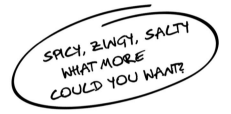

SPICY, ZINGY, SALTY WHAT MORE COULD YOU WANT?

INGREDIENTS
1 pineapple
1 lime
2 tsp caster (granulated) sugar
½ tsp cayenne pepper
1 pot of coconut yogurt
large pinch of salt

GET READY
sharp knife
chopping board
large plate/platter
grater
small bowl
teaspoon
4 serving plates

One for when you are being healthy but still want something sweet. This recipe is inspired by a Sri Lankan street food snack.

01 Slice the spiky top and bottom off the pineapple. Stand it up on its base, then carefully slice the skin off the sides and discard. Cut the pineapple into wedges and place on a large plate/platter. Discard the core if it's a bit tough.

02 Finely grate the lime zest into a small bowl. Add the sugar, cayenne pepper and salt and stir together. Sprinkle the spicy, salty, sweet mixture over the pineapple wedges. Serve straight away with plenty of cooling coconut yogurt on the side for people to help themselves.

SPEED HACK
As you cut the pineapple, put the wedges straight onto the serving plate/platter.

Dexys Midnight Runners
Come On Eileen

SERVES 4

ELDERFLOWER ETON MESS CHEESECAKE

INGREDIENTS

250 g (9 oz) full-fat cream
  cheese
1 tbsp elderflower cordial
150 ml (5 fl oz) double (heavy)
  cream
2 tbsp icing (confectioners')
  sugar
8 ginger nut biscuits
4 shop-bought meringue nests
150 g (5½ oz) fresh raspberries

GET READY

2 mixing bowls
tablespoon
whisk
large metal spoon/spatula
4 serving bowls

MOB, we've combined two classic puds here to make one beautiful bowl of smashed meringue, ginger nuts, raspberries and elderflower-flavoured cheesecake. It is epic.

01 Empty the cream cheese into one of the mixing bowls. Add the elderflower cordial and briefly whisk to loosen.

02 Empty the double cream into the other mixing bowl and add the icing sugar. Whisk until the cream just holds its shape – don't overdo it, you want it to be pillowy and light. Tip the whipped cream into the bowl with the cream cheese. Using a large metal spoon or a spatula, lightly fold the cream into the cream cheese in a clockwise motion. You want to try not to overmix or knock out the air, so four big turns with your spoon should do.

03 Crumble one ginger biscuit into the bottom of each bowl with your hand and crush three of the meringue nests between the four bowls. Tip the raspberries on top, then dollop over the cheesecake mixture. Crush over the remaining meringue nests and ginger biscuits to finish.

SPEED HACK
Crush the meringue nests and biscuits straight into serving bowls, then top each with one big dollop of cheesecake mixture.

INDEX

THANK YOU

I would firstly like to thank the genius behind all of the recipes in the book, Sophie Godwin. You have a sublime talent. It has been a total joy working with you and I couldn't be happier that you are now part of the MOB.

Next up, this book wouldn't have happened without the brilliant MOB Kitchen team; Michael, Alice, Felix, Dan, Sarah and Luca. This was a massive project and it wouldn't have been possible without such a brilliant group of people behind the business.

I would like to thank our brilliant photographer David Loftus. Your talent and skill is unrivalled, and it was an honour to work on a project with you. Ellie Silcock – the best food stylist in the world. Thank you. You brought the MOB touch and the food looks stunning throughout. Thank you also to Charlie Phillips with the best props. Last but by no means least, I would like to thank everyone at Pavilion – Cara, Polly, Helen, Laura and David for making this book happen. I am so proud to be part of the Pavilion family.

I would also like to thank my mum and dad for their constant support, my brothers Joe and Sam for their help and advice, and all of my best friends who have been on call at all hours of the day since MOB Kitchen began.

A special thanks goes to all my MOB who came to the book shoot – Paddy, Chester, Olivia, Hugo, Misha and Tommy.

I want to thank my amazing girlfriend, Robyn. Your support, at all hours of the day, is overwhelming. I was so happy you could be in this book! I love you.

Finally, I want to thank our brilliant design team, OMSE. James, thank you so much for your advice and help making the book look so beautiful!

Ben x